NO COUNTRY NO HOME

A Family's Exodus and Homecoming

by Trudy Walter Carlson

DORRANCE
PUBLISHING CO
EST. 1920
PITTSBURGH, PENNSYLVANIA 15238

The contents of this work, including, but not limited to, the accuracy of events, people, and places depicted; opinions expressed; permission to use previously published materials included; and any advice given or actions advocated are solely the responsibility of the author, who assumes all liability for said work and indemnifies the publisher against any claims stemming from publication of the work.

Dorrance Publishing Co
585 Alpha Drive
Pittsburgh, PA 15238
Visit our website at *www.dorrancebookstore.com*

ISBN: 978-1-6376-4374-7
ESIBN: 978-1-6376-4677-9

NO COUNTRY
NO HOME

A Family's Exodus and Homecoming

Acknowledgements

A special thanks to Amy Pearce because had she not asked to "borrow" my binders and notebooks, with all the paperwork I'd accumulated over the past twenty years, I probably wouldn't have been motivated to turn it into an organized manuscript.

Thank you to my "bosom buddy" Cindy Rurey for being a supportive and good friend since 1978. The years have been good to us.

A heartfelt thank you to my sister, Heidi Walter Schweitzer for the hours and hours she spent editing, making suggestions and laughing with me at some of the experiences we shared growing up in a German family.

Most important is my husband, Ernie Carlson for his unwavering love, commitment, continued support, and encouragement.

Legal Notes

This manuscript is a compilation of journals, interviews, and various documents such as birth certificates, birth entries in family Bibles, etc. The dates and places may not always be accurate as they were documented by individual family members. They were documented during extremely stressful and harsh circumstances and may not be 100 percent accurate in details, but their emotions and circumstances were.

All documents have been in my possession starting approximately twenty years ago and continuing up until the present day and were given to me by family members. Some of the documents are not dated and I needed to cross reference the information with other documents to verify the contents.

After my father's death, I was tasked with organizing and scanning hundreds of old and current photos – some of which were used in this manuscript. Some photos of maps, etc., have been in my possession for years and I don't know the origin, however, when possible, I obtained permission. I also downloaded non-family photos from a site, "Free photos of German refugees in WWII," because a picture is worth a thousand words in depicting the circumstances I was documenting.

None of these family photos, documents, journals, or any writings are to be used without my written permission.

Edelweiss
The Symbol of Honor and Hope

It was typical of a German citizen to have ivory-carved pendants of Edelweiss that would clip on a wide black ribbon to wear as a choker or bracelet or a brooch. For me, it was a beautiful symbol of Germany.

If you translate the word "Edelweiss," it means "noble" and "white." In the old days, men would venture out into the Alps to collect these flowers for their loved ones. Edelweiss was not always easy to get to, and sometimes these men would fall from icy ledges and snowy peaks. It was not uncommon to hear of men falling to their death trying to collect these beautiful flowers. If you were successful and able to bring these flowers home to your loved one, you were considered a brave man as well as one that risked his life to prove his love to his woman. This is the reason today that German men will proudly wear this flower. Unlike here in the United States, where wearing something flowered is considered unmanly, wearing this flower in Germany was like wearing a medal of honor!

Table of Contents

Introduction

Growing up, being part of a German/American family was an unequivocal way of life. My parents were extremely strict, and we only spoke German at home. English was not permitted. Over the years, that never changed. All our family friends were other displaced Germans, some of them arriving in America at the same time and on the same ship as we did. We attended a German school in Downtown Portland on Saturdays and a German church on Sundays – at least, we did until I became an embarrassment to my mother because I wouldn't behave.

After reading my Aunt Katherina and Uncle Adam's writings, and listening to my mom and dad's stories, it became evident to me that there was another side to our history that wasn't often talked about. We are inundated with stories about how invading Germans murdered millions of innocent people and destroyed villages across Europe, but little is said about how the average German citizen was treated under Hitler's rule.

Coming to America from a country with a different culture and language, wasn't easy. There was no button to press that instructed us "Push One for English, Push Two for German". There wasn't financial assistance, government assisted programs or health care offered to immigrants when we arrived. Nor was there anyone available to translate for us if we didn't understand what was being said. We were in America and we were expected to speak the language and adopt the culture. There was definite discrimination because we were German.

We had a sponsor who provided our family with room and board, but we were expected to earn our keep. We went to live on a ranch in Texas where my dad had to fulfill a two-year obligation to repay the farmer for our expenses and which also provided him a small salary. My mother was required to work in the main house.

It is no small wonder then, that we found comfort and safety in the company of other displaced Germans. They understood our culture, our challenges and spoke our language. We were accepted and not criticized or humiliated because we were German.

I know firsthand what it was, and still is, to be criticized and misunderstood simply because of the German culture and characteristics in our DNA and who we are. There's a T-Shirt that says, "I'm not angry – this is my German face" – that is an accurate description. I've been criticized many times for appearing to be angry when I'm not in the least bit angry. The older I get, the more my face tends to relax and sag into what looks like a frown.

I wanted to tell my family's story to let other WWII immigrant children know that they're not alone in their experiences of being criticized, misunderstood, and belittled because someone simply does not understand them. I'm immensely proud of being a German immigrant and grateful that I live in America.

Chapter One
Where It All Began

In the year 1365, German people were settling onto the land that would become Bukovina and Bessarabia. This land had previously been a protector of Chinese trade which resulted in German merchants and clergy working together to pave the way for other German settlers. These German merchants settled in the larger towns and communities, which paved a large role in establishing the Moldavian cities.

In the year 1745, Princess Sophie Frederika Auguste Von Anhalt, who was the daughter of an obscure German Prince, married Peter the Great, Czar of Russia. She became Catherine the Great of Russia in 1762 after her husband's death. Empress Catherine gained land, the result of two wars with the Ottoman Empire between 1768 and 1774 and the annexation of the Crimean Khanates in 1783.

Empress Catherine established a mint to encourage German workers with jobs and to aid the German migration to Russian territory. This settlement of Germans contributed to the full development of the land, resulting in a great migration of Germans and continuing into 1930, making the total number of German immigrants at this time 76,000.

Local villagers in Bessarabia gather for an afternoon celebration of singing and dancing. (Family Photos)

Chapter Two
Zorn Family

Catherine the Great encouraged her native Germans to migrate to Russia by distributing land among the German people and promising them work. As a result, the Zorn and Walter families, who originally came from Stuttgart, Germany, migrated to Bessarabia, Bukovina Russia in the late 1700s.

Every head of household received six hectares of land, which was equivalent to two and a half acres. When WWI started in Russia in 1914, the Zorn and Walter families were deported to Siberia because they were German citizens and not Russian citizens.

Great-Grandfather Heinrich Zorn, born in 1861 in Galicia, Austria, was a cabinet and furniture maker by trade so he was able to find work in a cabinet shop. It's interesting to note that Great-Grandfather and Grandfather were both named Heinrich Zorn. German families tended to use the same given name, sometimes giving the same names for other children using a different version (i.e., Heinrich Philipp Jacob Zorn would be the name of the first child, and the second child would be named Jacob Philipp Heinrich Zorn, etc.).

What is really confusing, and rather disconcerting, not to mention difficult when researching a family tree, is that when a child died, the birth of the following child was often given the same name as the child who died.

In 1884 Heinrich Zorn married Great-Grandmother, Eleanora Gross, also from Austria. My grandmother, Augusta Krohn, was born in Bessarabia in 1884 (d 1951) and helped support the family by being a maid for a wealthy Jewish Rabbi. The Krohn family had been captured by the Russians and deported from Wolienien, Russia. In 1915, the Zorn family was once again deported and sent to Siberia, which is where Grandmother Augusta met my grandfather, Heinrich Zorn who was born in Siberia in 1884 and died in 1979.

Grandfather Heinrich Zorn Sr. and Augusta Krohn were married in June 1917 in Siberia Russia, and in that same year, they were given permission to return to Bessarabia. Grandfather Heinrich Zorn's great-grandfather had twelve brothers and sisters and although we have never had it confirmed, we surmise that his family was of Jewish descent. After WWII, it was quite common for some Jewish people to deny their heritage to protect their family out of fear of repeated horrors.

They moved back to Czernowitz, Bukovina, until 1923, when they returned to Bessarabia and started a farm. They eventually owned forty hectares of land, two houses, and several unspecified large holdings. Katherina Zorn – Aunt Katherina –was born here in 1918, and Bertha Zorn was born in 1926.

Soon everything would change for the Zorn family. Starting in June of 1940, Russians took possession of Bessarabia letting Romanian soldiers move in to plunder and loot the villages and towns. Our family was forced to hide their livestock in hedgerows, ditches, shrubs, and thickets. A short time later that same year, Bessarabia was annexed to the Soviet Union. A treaty between the German and Soviet Union governments ensured the safety of those who were of German descent and guaranteed them safe conduct out of the country.

In 1940 Adolf Hitler sent out a proclamation for all Germans to return to Germany by October and fight for the "Fatherland". There were close to 93,500 Germans who answered Hitler's proclamation.

Note: "Fatherland was a nationalistic term used in Nazi Germany to unite Germans in the culture and traditions of their country."

Grandfather Heinrich Zorn didn't hesitate. He knew that because they were German settlers, they therefore had no rights in Russia, and their lands, houses, and goods would be confiscated by the Russians. They would be at risk of being sent to Siberia or other labor camps. It was with a heavy heart that Grandfather Zorn notified the authorities of his intention to return to Germany. The situation in Strembeni was too uncertain. The resettlement commission arrived to value the house, farm, and animals. They had to go, leaving everything behind. Since their passports verified that the family was German, returning to Germany was not a problem.

They were rounded up by German soldiers and loaded into large trucks, taking only what they could carry with them. They were transported to Romania where they were put on ships sailing to Yugoslavia, along with 80,000 other displaced Germans where they were housed in large tents. One of the large tents became the dining tent. Any documentation on the Germans from Southeastern Europe during the years 1939 to 1945 was practically non-existent, for official records had been lost or confiscated by the American and British governments.

For the next three days they received warm clothes and food for the children. They were divided up and transported to camps in Budweis, Boemen and Maeren. From Yugoslavia, they traveled to Austria where they were "welcomed" as belonging to the German Reich. Here they were faced with the reality of war and the hardships they would continue to endure.

By this time, it was winter, and the weather had turned bitterly cold. The family was determined to stay together even though there was little food available, and they were starving. Children and the elderly cried because of hunger. Whoever could work had to work. One day, Grandmother Augusta sent an open card to the officials in charge of the camp in which she detailed the situation they were living under. Immediately the conditions improved.

My grandparents and our family which at this time consisted of my grandparents, my mother, my aunt, and her children, resettled in Sudetenland which was the German name for areas of Czechoslovakia. Here they were housed in a school with 200 people grouped into five families living in one school room.

The young people were put on a train and sent to Gmunden, Austria to work, or they were recruited for the German military. Older men that owned horses and wagons had to go to Galicia, Austria where their horses and wagons were then confiscated. The men were put on trains and sent back to the camps. Many of these older men did not survive the arduous journey.

The Zorn, Walter, and Drummer families remained in this camp for a total of fifteen months until November 1, 1941, when they were then transported to Lodz Litzmannstadt, a much larger camp in Poland.

The Lodz camp was the second largest WWII camp and was referred to as a "ghetto" because it was in the poorest section of the city. Since it was surrounded by barbed wire and watch towers, it was totally isolated for 160,000 Jews and Romanians in German-occupied Poland. The families were again

5

resettled a few months later to Tuschenwald where two families received one house to share and survived on food brought in by the Wehrmacht, who were the army soldiers of the Third Reich. The food was packed in tubs, with one tub per household regardless of the number of people in each family. One day the tub might be turnip casserole and the next day it would be bean casserole, on a rotation.

In February of 1942, the Germans were resettled onto Polish farms. Each family had whatever household, personal, and farming tools the Polish families left behind. The resident Polish had to leave most of their belongings behind because the Germans were arriving within hours. Sometimes, all the furniture was still there, the hearth was still warm, and food was left in plates on the table. All their abandoned belongings and land were entrusted to these new German settlers. The "invading" German refugee families were given farm hands and maids to help with working the existing farms until 1943, when all remaining German young men were drafted into the military.

For weeks, it was known that the Russians were advancing into Poland. Covers were made for the wagons, bread was saved, geese and pigs were slaughtered, and larders filled with roasted meat. Down comforters and warm clothing were packed into trunks, and, on January 18, 1944, everyone was evacuated. It was a particularly cold winter and columns of horses proceeded day and night to Pomerania, East Germany, Mecklenburg and then to Ebsdorf and Stuttgart, Germany.

In 1945, the German refugees had to again flee, and leave the Polish farms where they were living, leaving everything they couldn't carry behind because the Russian invaders were coming. It was at this time that Great-Grandfather, Heinrich Zorn, threw up his hands in despair and said he could not take it anymore. He had a heart attack which resulted in his immediate death. His death devastated his family who now had to continue to flee from the Russians without his unwavering strength and support. The memory of his death would haunt my mother for years and cause her to relive the despair she felt at his loss.

Grandfather Heinrich and Grandmother Augusta, my mother and oldest sister were in Ebsdorf, Germany and were safe. As far as they knew, Aunt Katherina was on a train with her five children fleeing from the Russians. Her destination was unknown. Uncle Wilhelm was still a soldier, and Katherina's husband, Adam Drummer, and my father, Philipp Walter, were Prisoners of War. They were being held in separate POW camps.

Refugees were able to reunite with their families with the assistance of the International Red Cross who kept track of refugees. When a family arrived at the refugee camps, it was documented by the Red Cross and then again documented when they were transported to another destination. It made it possible for family members to find each other by following the trail created by these documents. The Red Cross also established auxiliary hospitals wherever possible and staffed them with Red Cross personnel. These hospitals were neutral and treated anyone unfortunate enough to be caught up in conflict.

Article 79 of the Geneva Convention allowed the Red Cross to pass on information or enquiries about refugees and POWs. They allowed a "letter" of up to twenty-five words and had to be about family news only. These messages were sent to the Red Cross headquarters in Geneva and then forwarded on to Red Cross locations throughout Europe. By 1945, twenty-four million messages had been exchanged.

After the Zorn, Drummer, and Walter families reunited in Ebsdorf, they had to once again find ways to survive. Grandfather Zorn earned money by transporting wood to the village wherever needed. Bertha and Katherina worked for a farmer milking cows and working in the fields. They received some money, potatoes, and sugar beets, and were able to save enough to buy a cow. They also had a previous farm hand who brought back two horses and a wagon, plus money from the sale of their colt, proceeds which were used to buy the cow. They had milk and butter and were able to get chickens and geese and raise them to provide for the family.

In 1946 there were settlements and apartments for refugees in Stuttgart, Germany. Since there was no longer any work available in Ebsdorf, the Zorn family members all moved to Stuttgart. Using money that Heinrich borrowed from a local bank, Grandparents Heinrich and Augusta Zorn bought a bought a bombed-out building on Strasse, Zuffenhausen, Baden-Württemberg, Germany. Katherina and her family, Wilhelm and his wife, Clara, and Bertha, Philipp and their daughter, Lydia, eventually all moved into this house and helped to restore and remodel it.

They first lived in near-by barracks in the Seedam Camp where Uncle Wilhelm had previously married Clara. Grandpa Zorn promoted this marriage because Clara came from a wealthy family, which provided some of the funds to facilitate the rebuilding of the apartment house.

Uncle Wilhelm shared with various family members that he went AWOL during the Allied invasion and Germany's surrender and worked his way through Poland. He miraculously found his sister, Aunt Katherina, at the train station as he made his way back to Germany. Wilhelm worked on Polish farms. When he arrived at a farmhouse, he would be able to work for food and a place to sleep and continue his way across Europe.

On one occasion, he got caught with one of the farmer's daughters, and he had to flee again because the outraged family notified the local authorities that Wilhelm was an escaped German SS officer. Wilhelm was on the run again. The family never wanted to talk about Wilhelm's participation as it was his choice to either become an SS Driver, or to become a soldier and get sent to the front. He didn't want to be in the middle of a war zone and wanted a safe and comfortable job driving an SS Officer.

Back Row: Bertha, Adam, Katherina with baby Rheinhold
Middle: Augusta, Lina and Heinrich Zorn
Front: Holdine Zorn, Reinhart and Eleanore Drummer
Bottom: Grandmother Augusta and Grandfather Heinrich Zorn. No idea who the rest are,
but they look good, don't they?

A family funeral – Heinrich Zorn is standing with his hand on the cross and Bertha Zorn Walter is on the right.

Grandfather Henrich Zorn and Augusta Krohn

Chapter Three
"Aus Unserem Leben"
Katherina Zorn Drummer In Her Own Words
Written by their son, Helmut Drummer
Translated into English by Lydia Walter Jensen

Katherina and Bertha Zorn as teenagers

I am Katharina Drummer, and I was born in Strembeni, Bessarabia in 1918. Both of my parents were held in confinement (also known as interned) in Russia from 1915 to 1918. My father's name is Heinrich Zorn, and he was born in Katharinendorf, Bukovina Russia. My mother is Augusta Krohn and met my father in 1917. When WWI ended, my parents moved to Strembeni,

Bessarabia in Romania, where my grandfather, Heinrich Zorn, and his family lived. My father had twelve brothers and sisters.

My mother's family came from an area called Schlesien, Germany. My mother had six brothers and sisters. When we first moved to Strembeni, we lived with my Aunt Katharina and paid her rent. This is where I was born on September 6, 1918.

In 1919 my parents moved to Czernowits, Bukovina where my father was a joiner, which is an artist and tradesman who builds things by joining pieces of wood such as ornamental work to hold furniture together. With the money he earned, my parents were soon able to buy a house in which they lived until 1923. In 1923, they moved back to Strembeni. They bought another house with land and began farming. In 1924 my brother Wilhelm was born, and in 1926 my sister Bertha was born.

During this period, we experienced a great famine and much suffering and, consequently, my father left us and went to Jaski, Russia to find work. During the next two years, he again worked as a joiner. He rarely came home, so my mother, sister Bertha, brother Wilhelm, and I had to work the land alone.

When my father was able to return home with his earnings, my parents were able to buy more land and soon we had forty hectares of farmland. We had servants, farm laborers, farm horses, six cows and forty to fifty sheep. One sheep alone could bring us a lot of profit because it provided us with lambs, wool, cheese and, eventually, meat. We harvested corn, wheat, rye, as well as sunflowers, rapeseed, soybeans, and watermelons. We grew grapes and made excellent wine. As children it was not unusual for us to have a glass of wine or a beer because the water in the villages was often contaminated and not safe to drink. Wine and beer were often the only choice.

Christmas was always a wonderful time. The whole family celebrated by attending the local church on Christmas. The entire village was in attendance as well. The children sang all the traditional German Christmas songs and read poems until, finally, the Christmas presents were passed out. Of course, we had the "Christollen" Christmas cake and we had dried wreaths that were covered with paper and candles were inserted. Candies, apples, nuts, cookies, and chocolate were our greatest treat and the essence of our celebrations. We were happy even without large presents. We were happy to receive home-made dolls, home-made cribs, or harmonicas.

New Year's was also a time of great celebration. In the evening we went to the church service with the entire village attending. At midnight, the church bells rang and, of course, guns were fired. We also had home-made fireworks. On New Year's Day all the children visited their grandparents and other relatives. Everyone wished each other a Happy New Year, sang songs, and received poems. We also received little gifts, mostly in the form of chocolate, sometimes a little money.

In Romania we used the Gregorian Calendar which meant that Romanians celebrated everything – thirteen days later. When we moved and registered in Romania, we had to change our birth date to allow for the thirteen-day difference.

Winter was a wonderful time. The harvest was finished giving us all a lot of time to meet with our friends in their homes. We sang, laughed, and danced. The boys entertained everyone while the girls were busy with crafts. It was also a good time to taste the wine we had made in the fall.

During the summer young people met in the village, went for walks, or met in the vineyards to taste the grapes. We could eat as much as we wanted to. Watermelons were a special treat that we enjoyed in the evenings. We would gather in front of our houses.

The village boys and young men played music on their accordions and harmonicas. We didn't have radios or current newspapers and spent a lot of our time sharing with each other whatever news we heard. Adam Drummer and Philipp Walter were each especially talented in playing the harmonica. Philipp also played the accordion while we sang German folk songs. I was in the school choir and later joined the church choir. I still remember a lot of songs from those days.

We had a teacher that taught us both German and Romanian. He also had a library. A book salesman visited our village, but I had no money for books. My mother sometimes gave me money so I could buy a book. What a joy it was to be allowed to buy a book. This joy of reading has passed on down through the generations of Zorn and Walter families.

In the meantime, my parents had opened a grocery store. No questions about it – I had to help there too. I was a salesclerk and had to make bags out of old newspapers and learned how to operate the scales. My father bought butter and I had to cut up the butter and then package it in smaller portions.

Once a week we had to sell the butter in the city which was thirty-three kilometers away.

We had to take the wagon and horses. Sometimes we were able to go along and help sell the butter, but that meant we had to get up at 5:00 A.M. We had some regular customers and were able to buy salt, sugar, rice, and other groceries the same day with the money we earned from the sales.

We had to be sure to remember petroleum for the oil lamps, otherwise we had to sit in the dark in the evenings. We gave our oil lamps special care. Every morning we had to clean the glass of the oil lamps, otherwise they would be too covered in soot from the burning oil. We cleaned them if we wanted to see anything the next evening.

We had many customs and traditions in our village of Strembeni. Among other things, the parents of the young people who were confirmed by receiving their rite of passage in the church, had to pay their way. Requirements were ten liters of wine, sausages, bread, and other foods had to be delivered. All these items were collected, and a big celebration was held.

Adam Drummer and I met at one of these celebrations. We had to keep our relationship a secret, especially from our parents. However, eventually my parents did learn of our relationship and I immediately received house arrest.

Despite the restrictions, Adam and I did manage to see each other every day. My father threatened to beat me if we continued to meet. He followed through on his threat and I did get beatings; however, the beatings had little effect on our growing love for each other. My father did not want me being involved with someone he didn't choose himself. I wasn't going to let anything stop me from being with Adam.

At the end of 1934, Adam received his notice to serve in the military and was ordered to report in early 1935. Adam insisted that we get married before he left for the military service which, of course, caused a lot of turmoil in both families. In the end, my father did finally consent to the marriage, saying, "Nothing seems to help. No one seems to be able to keep these children apart!" Therefore, in January 1935, at the age of seventeen, I got married, and on April 1, 1935 Adam had to leave for military service.

That's my dad, Philipp Walter standing up in the back.

Adam served in the Romanian artillery while I continued to live with my parents and work for them until Adam came back in December of 1935. At this time, we moved in with my in-laws where they gave us one room and was where our first child, Rheinart, was born on January 9, 1937. An heir to the name. Both grandfathers were immensely proud of their first grandson.

In the spring, Adam and I became independent of our parents and were able to build a house on a piece of land given to us by Adam's parents. The house had three rooms and stables for the cattle. We finally had our own home. As the firstborn son, Adam was the sole heir, and his sisters, Luise and Emilie, were already married.

From both his and my parents, we received four hectares of land, two horses, two cows and the basic tools for the farm. My father made us beautiful furniture for the bedroom, living room and kitchen. We were well off, and soon we were able to lease two more hectares of land giving us ten hectares of land to farm. We grew grapes for wine, sunflowers, wheat, and potatoes which we sold.

On June 14, 1938, God blessed us with our daughter, Elenore. At this time Adam was sick with an eye disease, drachma, so my father was the one who went to the courthouse and registered the birth of our daughter. Because my father's mother was called Elenore, my father named and registered our daughter as Elenore. Nobody asked us if that was what we wanted! We hadn't been able to pick out a name yet and resented that the decision was made by my father.

My grandparents were Christians and we enjoyed attending church services. Music and songs meant a lot to me, especially the songs about Jesus. That is probably why I enjoyed singing in the church choir. I learned to pray when noticeably young and believed that many of my prayers were answered. Everything went so well for us and we were happy.

WWII was well on the way. Soon, everything was about to change. The Russians took possession of Bessarabia. Romanian soldiers moved in and proceeded to plunder and loot the villages and towns. We had to hide our cattle in ditches, shrubbery, and thickets. A short time later, Bessarabia was annexed to the Soviet Union. A treaty between the German and Soviet Union governments ensured the safety of those of us who were of German descent and we were guaranteed safe conduct out of the country.

Adolf Hitler sent a proclamation to all German descendants telling us that those who wished to return to the Fatherland would be able to return to Germany by October 10, 1940, resulting in over 93,500 Germans answering Hitler's proclamation. With heavy hearts we notified the authorities of our intention to return to Germany because the situation in Strembeni, Bessarabia was too uncertain. The resettlement commission came to value our house, farm, and animals and we had to leave. We had to leave everything behind. We could only take what we could carry.

During this time Adam was called into the Romanian army as a reserve. However, when he heard about what was happening in Strembeni, he left at night without permission. He was in constant danger of being turned in, so he traveled by night through the forests and fields. Adam didn't want to be a soldier and wanted to return to what his previous life had been.

No sooner had Adam arrived in our village when he was turned in. The Romanian army searched everywhere for him. For two days he had to stay in hiding. Running away from the army usually meant certain death in front of a firing squad. We were never quite sure why Adam wasn't disciplined and was permitted to stay with us, but we knew better than to speak up.

As soon as the danger passed, we could organize our resettlement plans. When the time was up, women, children and older people were picked up and put in German military buses. The men left with the horses and wagons, and within two days our entire village was deserted while only the dogs remained to howl as we pulled out. This was the first time we left our belongings behind, our houses and land – everything of which we had been so proud.

The men had our provisions in the wagons. We had roasted meat, sausages, bread, packed up bedding, and clothing. We hoped to make the best of our situation and to save at least these few things. The disappointment was overwhelming, however; we heard that when the men reached Galicia – Romania on the Russian border – the authorities confiscated everything! The horses, the wagons, the food – all our provisions. Everything! We received a receipt and that was all. No money. Not one coin. That was difficult to accept. In the large square we could see hundreds of wagons – all confiscated. All our hopes for survival were shattered. We were not even allowed to keep our wagons.

The women, children, and the elderly reached Galicia where a large tent to serve as the kitchen was erected and everybody had to line up for their meals. How difficult it was for us to accept this situation. We were put on board ships along with thousands of other refugees and learned that we were going to Germany by way of Semlin, Yugoslavia. When we reached Semlin, large tents had already been erected and for a few days the authorities there took good care of us.

Again, we were torn apart. Adam had become extremely sick during the trip and was in a Red Cross hospital in Strembeni, Bessarabia where medical help was never denied, so we had to go on while he stayed behind. It was impossible to send him any news of our whereabouts. Again, we were faced with terrible uncertainty.

The Yugoslavians were very generous, and we received plenty of food and drink before being put on trains which took us to Graz, Austria. Austria didn't formerly exist as a country until 1938 when German troops marched in to annex the German country for the Third Reich. We were met with a great ceremony and speeches. We had come "home" to the Third Reich. The children received new clothes and were looked after, but we could feel that this was a time of war because of the soldiers and tanks. Everything was rationed and we were always on alert knowing everything could change in just a few moments.

Two days later we were on trains again and on our way to Budweis, Czechoslovakia, where we found shelter in an orphanage that was transformed into a refugee camp. A few days later, we again were sorted into groups and our family was sent to Suchental in Bohemia, Czechoslovakia. We were able to find shelter in a school with five other families living in one room. For one year we lived like this. My children and I received a bunk bed in one corner of the room. We received food rations in a large hall, which was the dining room where 250 people ate their meals.

When I was nine months pregnant with my third child, and, because there was no doctor in the camp, I had to go back to Budweis. I left Rheinart and Elenore behind in the camp together with my parents. Rheinart was now three years old and Elenore was two. Now, for the first time, I was separated from my children. I still had no news regarding Adam, and it was important to me to try and find out anything I could. I was distraught at having to leave my children behind with my parents, but it would not have been safe for them and it would have been harder for me to travel.

News at last! I learned that Adam was still in the hospital, where sickness and a cold had left him quite ill, and he and a few other patients were transferred to Budweis where he was able to meet up with his sister, Emilie, and her family. Was it accidental that Adam and I were in the same city at the same time? It was destiny and, for us, it was an unexpected miracle. We were together again.

After months of being separated, we were together again with the one goal to get back to our children. We contacted the camp personnel and asked for permission to go back to Suchental, Czechoslovakia and when permission was granted, I was able to return to my parents' home and be with my children. This was Christmas in 1940, and on Christmas Eve, our family was together again. A wonderful Christmas despite the unpleasant circumstances.

In January 1941, our Hilda was born in the camp. Times were still exceedingly difficult, especially for the baby. I could not nurse her because we had so little to eat and there was nothing, absolutely nothing for a baby. The Czechoslovakian camp authorities were not inclined to help us. Mercilessly, they let us beg for milk or tea.

Along with many other children in the camp, Hilda became extremely ill with a lung infection. A doctor came to the camp. The children with communicable diseases were interned in a separate room. The doc was particularly concerned for Hilda and called her his "problem child." I prayed to God for the health of my child and soon she started getting better.

In November of 1941, we were transported to another camp in Litzmann-stadt in Poland. This camp was in a forest that consisted of what had previously been holiday cabins. Together with my in-laws we were given a cabin with bunk beds, a table, four chairs and a coal stove. All this was for seven people. We stayed there that winter until February of 1942. It was cold, and we received very few coals for the stove and the men would get together and go into the forest to find wood.

We received food from the military personnel and every morning a pail of tea was placed in front of our house along with bread and margarine. For lunch we would receive a pail of stew with sugar beets or carrots. In the evenings it would be a pail of tea with bread and we always made sure to hurry outside to get our food when it arrived because otherwise it would be stolen. We had not yet received any food coupons and we were always hungry.

In February 1942, we were relocated to farms and transported in buses. None of us knew what to expect until we reached our designated farms. It was cold and the farmland was covered with snow. The house was empty and when we entered the house we found, much to our surprise, that the house was still warm. The authorities had only that very morning transported the Polish family that owned the farm to a refugee camp. This was quite an oppressive feeling! The Polish families in the village were forced to leave because the Germans were coming.

After two weeks we had a visitor. A young teenage boy arrived on our doorstep telling us he was the son of the former owners and asked if he could work for us as a servant. Of course, we took him in. The farmhouse was old and consisted of three rooms and a kitchen.

My mother- and father-in-law had one room and we used the other two rooms. We prepared our meals together in the kitchen. The farm consisted of sixteen hectares of land, two horses, three cows, and two pigs. Slowly our standard of living began to improve.

We began to receive food coupons and were able to give our children enough to eat. We butchered one of the pigs and received furniture from a United Nations Aid Organization (Nationalen-Cersorgungs-Hilfe NSV).

Because the house was full of mites and rats, we had a lot of hard work ahead of us and it took weeks to cleanse the house of vermin. By summer, the house was completely clean and in May of 1942, our son named after his father, Adam, was born. We were now a family of six and had a servant, Herman, and a maid, Brunja, as well as Stefan, the son of the former owners.

Life was much better. We worked on the land and the harvest was good and we managed to raise geese, turkey, ducks, and chickens. The stables were filled with pigs, six cows and several calves. The tax authorities demanded quite a bit from us but left us with enough from which to live. We were now ten people at a well provisioned table at mealtimes.

Even though the authorities didn't allow servants to eat with the owners (it was strictly forbidden), Stefan, Herman and Brunja ate at the same table with us. On one occasion, the authorities came on a surprise visit and found us all together at the table; they gave us a severe warning. However, my father-in-law stood firm and said, "Whoever works with me, eats at the same table with me." That was his rule, and nothing would change it.

It was up to the lady of the house to provide the bread – this was viewed as a measure of her abilities. First, the dough had to be good if the bread was to be good. Then the temperature of the oven was critical. We heated the ovens with wood and corn cobs. The temperature had to be exact, but we had no thermostat. We tested the heat of the ovens with the back of our hands. If the oven were not hot enough, the bread remained unbaked and, if it were too hot, the bread burned.

We had to build our own bread oven from bricks made from clay. The oven we built was long enough for twelve round loaves of bread. After the baking we heated the ovens again to make "Streusselkuchen" also known as crumb cake and is made of yeast dough covered with a sweet crumb topping that we call streusel. Streusel is made of sugar, butter, and flour. It's delicious! At Christmas we baked cakes and cookies and sometimes we baked two or three baskets full of treats. For weddings we baked the meat in this oven.

We would prepare chickens with rice, potatoes with meat in pots, and baked in the oven. We built this oven outdoors in a summer hut; otherwise, it would have the inside of the house unbearably hot.

In November of 1943 our son, Frederik, was born. My husband, Adam, was still home but everything indicated that he would soon be called back into the military and within twenty-four days, we received the news. Adam was called to the front lines in France.

Once again, we said goodbye to each other with neither of us knowing how things would turn out. I stayed behind on the farm with our five small children. My father-in-law became ill and was unable to recover and died in July of 1944, and then my mother-in-law left to live with her daughter, Luise, and I remained on the farm alone with the children. Our faithful servants and maid served me well during this difficult and critical time.

Rumors flew again. The Russians were getting closer all the time and it looked like we would have to pack up and flee again. I received a letter from Adam telling me he was in a military hospital in Zerbst. I was devastated. Should I try to get to Adam? Could I leave the children behind? In my great need I prayed to God for a sign. I also asked our neighbors for advice and they immediately offered to look after my children and the farm. I took this as a sign of consent from God and in January 1945, I took the train to Zerbst and stayed with Adam for two days in the military camp. On January 8, I was back home with my children again.

Once again Adam was put back in the military and had to leave. Refugees were leaving and, once again, we realized that we would have to prepare for departure. Our servant, Herman, prepared the wagon for our flight. We butchered and roasted geese and a pig in a preservative for the trip. I baked bread and zwieback which was a sweetened bread enriched with eggs that is baked and then sliced and toasted until dry and crisp making it a very sustainable and welcome bread and was included when we packed the wagon.

In the middle of the night our neighbor knocked on our window and told us it was time to flee again. Helpless and alone, I stood there. The children were sleeping so soundly in their beds. I woke Reinhart first and then Elenore and, because I had already prepared them for the trip, they knew what to do.

We woke the other children, dressed them, and prepared the last warm meal they would have for quite some time. We finished packing the wagon with any remaining provisions and loaded the children. Our wagon followed other wagons in their flight. Rheinart was eight years old; Elenore was seven, Hilda was four, Baby Adam was two and a half, and the baby, Frederik, was fifteen months old.

Herman harnessed the horses and took us to Rippin, Poland. Because all the roads were congested with refugees, we decided to continue our trip by train. At the train station in Rippin, it was the same confusion. The trains that arrived were already overcrowded but we had to get on! I pushed my children into the train through the window and pushed myself in through the door at the end. All our provisions, the wagon, the horses had to stay behind. Once again, we found ourselves with no more than what we had in our pockets and on our backs.

My first goal was to find my children in the crowded train. We got separated in the confusion and crowds after I pushed them through the window and had to run around to the back to get in. I found them all except for Elenore. Desperate and distraught, I continued searching. I found her pressed under a bench, motionless and almost suffocated. I pulled her out and she revived. Finally, the train started to move, and outside people were crying and screaming as they were being left behind. The scene was horrendous and one I will never forget.

After a little while, I recovered from the fear and terror and began to look around in the compartment. I could not believe my eyes as I saw a friend that I had known for years, on the train with her four children also in our compartment. What a joy in the middle of such terrible confusion. A blessing from God.

During the trip, the train stopped in an unknown place. I still had my food coupons and I wanted to go into town to try and get some food for my children, but no one knew how long the train was stopping. I had no choice but to ask God to please let the train wait until I was able to get some food. Completely trusting in God, I left my children and ran as fast as I could into town, bought some food and ran back. I had not quite reached the train when it started to move. In desperation I kept running and jumped on barely in time. I found my children and I was able to give them some food.

My friend and I discussed our situation and tried to find out where the train might stop next. We were told it would be in Karthaus and collecting our children, we decided to leave the train. After another three hours the train stopped, and we got off. Through the Red Cross, I had the address of a family called Leimert, and with the help of the police, Father Leimert was informed that we had arrived.

We waited for hours until he came with his wagon and horses and picked us up. My friend and her children were picked up by her sister who lived nearby. The Leimerts had twelve children of their own as well as both sets of grandparents living with them but didn't hesitate to take us in, give us a room, and share their food with us.

However, we were unable to find rest here for long. The Russian front continued to move in, and we could hear the cannons rumbling in the distance and knew we could not stay here for much longer. No one knew when, what to do or where to go.

Where was Adam? There was no mail, and I had no way of letting him know where we were. A few days later some people from Danzig arrived and came to visit the family we were staying with. I begged them to take a card to Adam and mail it from Danzig. I never gave up hope. I thought maybe the mail was still in service in Danzig and maybe, just maybe, Adam would receive the card letting him know where we were.

Days of uncertainty and fear were to follow. The situation in Karthaus became more and more dangerous. We had to barricade our doors out of fear for retribution from the Russian sympathizers.

One evening while sitting in the dim light of an old carbide lamp, we heard a knock at the door. We sat in total fear and refused to answer the knock. The knock came again, and again, and again. Finally, Father Leimert called out "Who's there?" and the answer came back "Do you know anyone named Adam Drummer?"

It would be impossible to describe our joy as Adam stepped into the room and embraced us. God had helped our little family and reunited us. How could this possibly have happened? Adam had received the card I sent while he was in the military hospital.

He showed the card to the military doctor who allowed him to leave for seven days to help bring his family to safety. Seven days of leave in the middle of the war. Another miracle.

However, regardless of our joy, Adam brought us back to reality. We had to leave because the Russians were moving closer and he had to return to the military. Once again, we had to pack up as we had been doing for so many years. Father Leimert took us with his horses and wagon to Lauenburg train station. The train station was full of desperate refugees. When a cattle train arrived, we got on and sat on the straw that was laid down on the floor of the train. There were no lights or toilets but at least the train was moving.

In Pomerania we found lodging in a sports hall and we managed to find a spot near the door. We put the children on the bare floors and covered them with our coats while we considered what our options were. We went to the United Nations Aid Organization where they told us if we had relatives in the German Reich, we could buy train tickets to Germany and there was a train leaving that very night for Hamburg.

Adam and I looked at each other and said to each other, "If only we had relatives in the Reich." I suddenly heard a voice, as clear as if someone were sitting right next to me, saying, "You have a relative in Stuttgart. His name is Adam Krohn." That was my uncle!

We immediately went to the ticket counters and told them we had an uncle in Stuttgart, but nobody knew where that was. The officials looked at a map and found Ebstorf which was near Luneburg. They told us that we needed to hurry, because at one o'clock, the train would arrive. We scraped together the last bit of money and bought the train tickets. We gathered up our children and returned to the train station.

The train arrived and was completely overflowing with refugees leaving us a small place out on the platform as the only free spot. We climbed on and I stationed myself at the back and the children in the middle covered with our coats while Adam stood on the stairs to the platform and held on to the bars with both hands. That is how we traveled all night in February in the bitter cold, but we didn't complain because the train was moving.

Towards morning, the train door opened and in the compartment were psychiatrists from the Storgard. When they saw the children, they let us into the compartment, and we were able to sit on luggage and crates and we were appreciative that we were now warm. That is how we arrived in Hamburg. Two of my children, Frederik and Adam were sick.

In Hamburg we received nourishment before continuing with the next train to Ebstorf. We arrived in Ebstorf at six in the morning. We rang the bell and the station master allowed us to get off the train and go into the waiting room where we laid our children on the benches and waited while the officials contacted the police. Shortly after the call we received the exact address of our relatives that was a thirty-minute walk from the train station. At seven in the morning, we were on our way. Rheinart had to stay behind to look after the children as he had done so often during the last several months.

With great trepidation we knocked on the door and after my uncle opened the door, he took one look at me and shouted "Katherina! Where in the world did you come from? Your parents had given you up and they are here with us as well. They have a house and room for all of you!" Immediately we were taken to our parents' house on Hohenlohe Strasse.

The surprise and joy we felt at this news was overwhelming and my father set off to the train station immediately to get our children. We received a room, beds, and a change of clothes because my parents had been able to get through to Germany with the wagon and horses and all their provisions. Thanks be to God and His great help!

Once again, we knew Adam would have to leave and the day of his departure grew closer and closer. Just months away from the end of the war, on March 9, 1945 he was called to Vienna. He was then sent to the Eastern front, and on April 18, he was wounded and transported back to the military hospital in Regensburg, Germany. From there in May 1945 when the war ended, he was sent to an American prison camp. My two children, baby Adam and Frederik were not able to recover from their illness and both died within hours of each other. Without Adam at my side, I was alone and discouraged as I stood by their shared grave.

I needed to help provide food for my family, I started work on a local farm where I received milk and potatoes for my labor. It was not much but was enough to feed the children. In June, another miracle occurred when our former servant, Herman, arrived from Poland. With our wagon and horses, he and other refugees had managed to get as far as Ludwigslust where he located my father who told him where to find me.

Herman continued his journey with the wagon and horses. He had come through with one bag of flour which he presented to me with great flair. "Ma'am, here is your wagon, horses and DM 300. I sold the foal during the trip and here is the money I received. I'll work until I have enough money for the return trip to Poland." He was able to leave us a short while later and returned to his homeland.

What a tremendous help Herman had provided. I was able to sell the horse and bought a cow instead. Farmer Kotke, who owned the farm where I worked, allowed us to keep our cow in his field. At night, the cow went into the stable together with his cows and all were fed. In exchange I helped with the milking twice a day.

I took the flour Herman had brought me to the baker and was able to pick up one loaf of bread each day. Farmer Kotke took the second horse I had and used it on his farm, where it was also fed and looked after. I was obliged to deliver twenty liters of milk each day, however, I was permitted to keep three to four liters. In exchange for the milk delivery, I received two kilograms of butter each month, which was a great help for all of us.

During this turmoil, the International Red Cross played an important part in helping families keep track of each other. As we arrived in different camps throughout Europe, we always checked with the Red Cross giving them our names, how many and who was in our group and where we were. When we left an area, we once again went to the local Red Cross and let them know where we were going. By doing this, families were able to locate family members.

Because of this, my sister Bertha arrived with her little daughter, Lydia, and moved in with us. Her husband, Philipp Walter was still in an American prison camp.

In May 1945, the war was over! What a relief even though our husbands were still in prison camps and being held by the Americans. We were hopeful that they would soon be released.

Adam was released from the prison camp on July 10, 1945 and through the Red Cross, was able to find us. He was quite ill and was an invalid and unable to work. By August he had recovered enough to take our wagon and horse to deliver wood to the local farms. A short while later, he was employed by the State to work in the forest. We sold the horse and bought clothes and shoes for our children. Rheinart and Eleanore went to school. Slowly, very slowly, our lives improved.

Our daughter, Erika, was born on May 5, 1946 and Adam lost his job. My parents moved to Stuttgart, Wurttemberg, Germany. They sent us a letter asking us to come to Stuttgart and said Adam could find work there. After living in a refugee camp in Zuffenhausen in Wurttemberg, Germany, Grandfather Zorn was able to buy a bombed-out house and started to rebuild it. He encouraged us to come help rebuild the house to provide a home for all of us. In May 1949, Adam left for Stuttgart and began to help my father rebuild the house. Three months later he was able to get a job at Stuttgart-Feuerbach, which is a district of Stuttgart.

In 1949 while I was still in Ebstorf, an evangelical revival took place. I was invited and attended the meeting and became a convert. As a child, I always attended church services that took place in the home of my grandparents and I had learned many songs from my mother. I now reached an important decision that would be a turning point in my life.

Together, with other Christians, we held services in our own home. We became friends with the Vogt family and an eighteen-year-old young man named Rheinard Ulonska and I have many wonderful memories of all that we shared.

In November 1949, my children and I were able to move to Stuttgart where we moved into an unfinished apartment in the half-finished house my grandfather had bought. The floors and doors were not yet installed, but we were happy and back together again as a family. My mother, Augusta Krohn Zorn, told me of church services in the Hohenstein School. She had attended the church services there and found them very comforting.

The very next Sunday we searched for the Hohenstein School, and from that time on, these services became an integral part of our lives. Adam was the first to accept Christianity and then my sister, Bertha, her husband, and finally my father. Our children followed our examples. We were a happy family and singing together became an important part of my life. Rheinart learned to play the mandolin and accordion, and Elenore and Hilda played the guitar. In the meantime, we welcomed another addition to our family in 1954 when Helmut was born.

Rheinart became friends with some of the young men at the Hohenstein School and helped start the missionary work in Zuffenhausen. We became a part of this from the very beginning, and the first meeting for this youth organization began in our kitchen in a rebuilt house on Hohenloher Strasse.

It started out with only young men and before long, young women joined the group. Our kitchen became a meeting place for everyone, including our generation. Through these meetings the trumpet players began to meet with Gunter Hageloch being the leader. Rheinart concentrated and taught him, as well as others, to play the trumpet and became the director for the group. There was no question about where the group would practice – our home, of course! Adam would often flee to our vineyard during the practice sessions.

Our apartment was small – thirty-seven square meters. We had a little bedroom and a small living room. The largest room was the kitchen, and we shared the toilet in the hall. Later we were able to add a small bedroom for the children. We felt rich. We loved our large kitchen where our family spent time together. Many conferences took place here and we often had guests for several days.

Some of these visiting guests were Gerhard Zucker who stayed with us for four years while he studied. Ewald Mayer lived with us for two years, Emilia Lukas was with us for two years, and Alma Freiberg one year. We frequently had visitors and guests who dropped in. The country was still very unsettled with many German citizens not able to locate their families or former homes sometimes for years. Strangers were always there to take them in for as long as it was needed. There was nowhere else for them to go. It was a wonderful and fulfilling time in our lives and many friendships date back to those days. In later years, our church was built in the Gugliner Strasse 4, and the services and meetings moved to the church.

In 1950, we decided to emigrate to America and together with my sister, Bertha, and her family, we applied for immigration. We received notice and were requested to appear before the immigration authorities in Hanau, twenty-five miles to the north of Frankfurt. We were interviewed, questioned, and prepared for possible acceptance in three weeks. Then came the news. My sister and her family could immigrate to the United States, but we were rejected when the doctors had found a scar on one of my lungs during the required physical. It was quite a surprise since I had no symptoms or problems. After six months we were again called in for an interview but again, were rejected.

A year passed after we applied for our emigration when Gunter Hageloch came to our door and asked if he could pray with us. He wanted to pray that God wouldn't let us leave Germany, and we agreed to pray with him. We applied one more time, but this time it was to emigrate to Canada. My sister, Bertha, was extremely homesick and was begging us to come. Our application was rejected again, and we knew with certainty, that it was God's will that we remain in Germany and cancelled any plans we had to leave Germany.

Chapter Four
Adam Drummer In His Words

I am Adam Drummer and I have always been a farmer. My parents, Jakob and Mathilde Drummer, were overjoyed when I arrived: their son and heir. I was the sole heir to the farm and lands, even though I had two sisters who were older than I was. I was born in November 1913. As a six-year-old, I had to work on the farm, and everybody had their specific jobs. Mine was to ride the horses when we plowed the fields and to help with the harvesting. I had to help bring in the harvest with the wagons. Working on the farm was hard work.

By the time I was thirteen, after we brought in the harvest with wagons, my job was to lead the horses at the threshing. We worked in temperatures of forty degrees and this work was not fun. Evenings were spent shoveling the harvest away from the threshing machine, which is where the grain was separated from the hulls during the thrashing. We were able to get in a few hours of sleep before filling the sacks with the grain and carrying them to the loft to be stored.

Harvest time meant weeks of back-breaking work until all the grains, rye, oats, wheat, soybeans, and sunflower seeds were brought in and stored. During harvest and, later, when we gathered the grapes, the whole family worked, including all the children. Only the pumpkin harvest was a joyful occasion. We harvested many pumpkins, and we were able to keep the seeds. We dried the seeds and sold them. That was the only pocket money we ever had. Otherwise, Christmas and New Year were times when we received a little money from our parents. Living on a farm, we had little time to go to school and even less time to do schoolwork.

Our parents provided us with clothes and a trousseau, depending on their income. Our mother earned money from the fowl she raised and sold, as well as from the sale of eggs and butter. From the profits of the harvests, we bought seeds for the following year. We bought clothes, shoes and linen from the money that was left at the end of the year. If we had a good harvest, we indulged in luxuries. Sometimes there was enough money for a wristwatch!

We were stationed in Bonn/Rhine and took turns on watch. American air strikes hit us constantly and in 1944, a devastating air strike destroyed the entire city center. My watch had just ended, and my relief had just shown up when suddenly the sirens sounded. American bombers. And the bombs were already flying without giving us enough time to reach cover. To the right of me a bomb hit a building and splinters were flying and hitting me. I fell to the ground with splinters striking me in the head and arms and, as a result, I was taken to the military hospital. It took me more than four weeks to recover and to get back on my feet. Many splinters are still in my body and are a painful reminder of that bomb attack.

After my recovery, I was sent to the feared Eastern front in the vicinity of Vienna, which was not far from the Russian front. The Russians were well camouflaged in a section of the forest directly in front of us. Between the Russians and us was a mere 400 meters of open area. It was a death sentence for us when we were ordered to cross and attack. We began to cross the open area while the Russians sat in the trees and shot us down like rabbits.

We didn't have the slightest chance of crossing alive. Seventy of us moved forward and seven had already turned back when the order came to retreat. I was shot. Like a snake crossing the open field I tried to avoid the bullets and get back to cover, however, when I did a deathly sight met me. Most of my comrades lay on the ground wounded and dying while my injury was an upper thigh wound.

We hid out in an old barn for days knowing we had little chance of being rescued while the Russians continued to bombard us with bullets nearly shooting the roof off. There was no possibility of getting transport to get out safely. Our chances of survival became less by the minute, however, miraculously an old truck appeared to help to get us out. Without mercy we were piled into the back of the truck where we lay helplessly next to or on top of each other.

Only three of us survived the trip to the military hospital. We barely recovered before we were transported to an American prison camp in 1945 located in Regensburg, Germany that was the site of the largest "Displaced Persons" camp in Germany.

We didn't receive any food or drink the first four days and it rained day and night and, without having any shelter, we stood in mud and water. We were hungry and the rain provided the only drink available. Sickness broke out and spread rapidly before a few of us were called up to head out. About 1,600 of us were moved and I was one of them.

The conditions became a bit more tolerable and we had shelter in tents in a camp along the river. It was two people in each tent. We still had infrequent and small amounts of food. In the mornings we received a loaf of bread for fifty men providing us with a small piece of bread for each of us. At lunch we received soup and another loaf of bread for fifty men to share. We were in this camp for four weeks suffering from severe hunger and homesickness, and not getting any word from our families.

One day, we suddenly received an order. Those of us whose wounds had not completely healed were to come forward and be the first to be released. My companion who shared the tent with me threatened to hit me over the head with a hammer (I do not know where he would have found a hammer!) if I didn't come forward.

I came forward. When the doctor checked on me, he saw the scars on my arm. He immediately contacted the commander of the camp because he thought I had been an SS officer and had removed the SS tattoo. I faced the threat of severe punishment and imprisonment. Fortunately, I had documentation through my soldier's papers that I had never been an active member of the SS.

As a result, my young companion and I were among the first to be released. However, we could not be released into the American sector where my family was but were released to a farmer in the area. The farmer took us in and allowed us to stay with him for three days. My companion kept pressing me "Come on, let's get going," even though I could hardly walk, so I was hesitant. My companion insisted that we would manage, so we left the farm not knowing how we would ever be able to get into the American section.

All the bridges were being watched and every passerby's paperwork was verified. We stood in front of a bridge and were unable to go any further. Out of nowhere, an American jeep came towards us and stopped. The soldiers got out and asked where we were going. Using our hands and feet, we tried to explain that we were trying to enter the American zone.

The soldiers helped us get into their jeep and took us quite a distance in the direction we wanted to go. That is how we were able to cross the bridge without inspection and passed the guards to get into the American sector. The friendly Americans helped us out of the jeep on the other side of the bridge and we were able to continue our journey.

We stopped at a bakery and begged for bread, then at the butcher's we begged for a little sausage to go with our bread and somehow managed to survive. Farmers allowed us to sleep in their stables and after eight long days, we reached our destination and I saw Katherina working in the garden. What a sight I must have been. I was dirty, tired, extremely thin and limping badly because of my injury but she finally recognized me. How great was our joy!

Chapter Five
Bertha Zorn Walter

In German, my name is Bertha, and in German it is pronounced as Berta (pronounced Bear-ta). I raised five children. I was born in Strembeni, Bessarabia on January 1, 1926 and had a good life. My mother and my father had a large farm and owned a large store where they were able to sell their own farm products. We had a lot of domestic help and farmhands to work both inside and outside of our house. It was a particularly good life.

In early 1940 we heard that the Russians were going to come in and take over our country. There were about 93,000 Germans who lived in Bessarabia at that time. Our village of Strymbeni was not noticeably large. My mother and father spoke fluent Russian, Romanian, Yiddish – not Hebrew but Yiddish – and fluent German. My mother's folks were from Germany and my father's parents were from Austria.

When the Russians took over our village, they took everything we had. Everything. We were not sure what day they would arrive on our doorstep, but we knew they were coming. My mother and father were sure that they would never come into the house, but they did, and they took over our home and our village.

At that time, we had two houses. One house was for summer and one for winter. We were prepared and kept the kitchen windows open and when they came and knocked on our door, we immediately went out the windows and hid in the orchards. They confiscated both our houses and moved in. They slaughtered whatever livestock they could get their hands on. After that we were never free from the fear of not knowing what would happen to us.

A couple of days later, on June 28, 1940, Germany made an agreement with Russia. The Russians said that the Germans could move out and Hitler sent in troops to evacuate us for only one reason. Hitler wanted to remain in power and at that time Germany didn't have many tanks and they needed a lot of horses. My father was able to leave with the horses, but my mother and the rest of us were taken away on buses.

We were taken away on those buses into Yugoslavia and they had tents for us. Big tents are where they put us and provided us with enough food to eat and have shelter.

Later, we were gathered, then grouped for transportation into Austria. In Austria we were housed in a big monastery that looked down on the village about a half a mile below. At that time, we were about 250 refugees. There were about five families per room. In the beginning they gave us enough food, but after a week's time, we were not getting any more provisions, food or water. The food ran out and we were unable to leave and get more because all the monastery doors were locked. We were locked in and nobody in the village below knew we were there. The troops that had moved us two weeks previously locked the doors on our arrival, and they didn't tell anybody we were there.

After a few days, my mother said "come downstairs with me. I'm going to try to get a message to my brother in Germany so my family will know what happened to me and how I died." When my mother and I went down to a lower floor, we were able to find an unlocked window. We were able to push the window open enough so my mother could lean her head out and shout to a passerby below (we were in Austria and everyone spoke German), asking if he would send the message and he didn't hesitate.

So off he went, and we went back upstairs. It was approximately thirty minutes later that we heard banging on the front door, a group of us ran down to the front hall to let them know we were locked inside. Someone on the other side of the door shouted back to us and the villagers were able to break down the door and come in.

A man asked us, "Who wrote that card?" and my mother said, "I did." And he said, "Is this true? Have you been without food?" And everybody shouted, "Yes! Yes! Yes!" The villagers left and promptly came back bringing us food and water and were able to save all of us from starvation.

The villagers notified the authorities about our situation and location. We were kept at the monastery for another two weeks before being transported to a different location in Czechoslovakia. We were put in a schoolhouse and all 250 of us were packed with several families together in one classroom with bunks. I slept next to my brother and my mother slept next to my sister. My younger sister and I had to scoot sideways to get into our bed because the room was so crowded. We stayed there in that crowded room for weeks. I was fourteen.

It was so crowded in there and what food we were given was not good. We did not get enough for everyone and many of the children got sick. My little sister, Holdine, got quite sick and was removed from our camp and we didn't know where they had taken her. We were told she had diphtheria which meant they had to isolate her. After several weeks of not knowing how or where she was, I told my mother that I was going to go to town and find my sister.

I went to the overseer of our camp and asked him if he would allow me to go to work and he found work for me. We got a couple of girls together and at 5:00 A.M. the next morning we walked a mile to the train station and got onto the train near the Austrian border. We got off the train at the next village and from there walked another mile to a factory where we were able to work.

On the way home I told my companions that I was going to find a hospital or an orphanage where they keep refugee children without families because I was sure that's where my little sister was. I found a hospital close by with little sheds lined up in back, but the fence was made of wire and it was six feet high. I found a place that I could pry open and was able to squeeze through. I went through and started looking in every little shed to find my sister.

I started looking through the little sheds. They all faced the main building, and I didn't want to get caught so I got behind them and was able to look through the windows until I found her. When she saw me, she screamed my name. She had not had any contact with family for weeks. They had kept her isolated and when she saw me, she became excited and screamed and screamed while I motioned to her to be quiet.

She kept screaming until one of the nuns came in and saw me in the window. She rushed around the shed and grabbed me by the arm and demanded, "How did you get in?" I told her it was through the chicken wire. I had pried it open with my hands because I wanted to find my sister. I told her that my mother is so upset she cannot sleep. I told my mother that I would search until I found her. I firmly planted my feet on the ground and refused to move. I had found my sister and I wasn't going to go anywhere.

The nun asked me where I lived so I told her it was in a camp a long way away and this was the only chance I had to get out. She said to come back in through the same hole in the fence and she would watch for me and help me to be able to see my little sister.

When I started working at the factory every day the owner's son brought me an orange that was wrapped so nice. I had never seen an orange before but I knew it was special so I asked the nun if she would give the orange to my sister, and she did.

Aunt Holdine, my mother Bertha and older sister Lydia

During the war Czechoslovakia was a major manufacturer of machine guns and artillery. I worked in a factory until I got hurt. We worked on big machines that were not meant to be used by young girls and I got hurt using one of them. I was so very tired and got little food in the camp. I was so very tired and hungry and didn't have enough strength to operate the machines and ended up getting hurt.

We spent a year in that camp until they loaded us all up again, taking us to a different camp hidden in the woods with lots of little cabins. It was April and still cold. In the morning they brought each of us a milk can with tea, a slice of bread with a little butter on it. At lunch they brought another can to us with soup, sometimes with a few potatoes but usually it was cabbage. In the evening we got the same bread and tea. It was not nearly enough but that is what they gave us.

One day, while I was standing in the kitchen of our little cottage it suddenly got dark and I was scared. I looked out and there was a big tank parked right in front under the window and two soldiers got out of the tank and started walking towards our little cottage and we were terrified. We didn't know if they were Russians, Germans, Americans or the British.

We were so afraid because the Russians were very cruel. We gathered and pushed into a little space behind the stove where we stacked the wood. It was

39

very crowded, and we had to be very quiet. We could not find the door to go out to the shelter across the street at the schoolhouse and we were unable to locate the escape door that would lead us out.

We pushed and pushed each other until we all fit into the tiny space when suddenly we heard grenades and mortars exploding as they crossed over and landed on the ground both in front and behind our house. Our terror was so intense that we didn't know how to react and if we were able to even breathe.

My mother said there was something bad going on outside and she was able to peek out and saw that the soccer field in front of the schoolhouse was now a battlefield with our house being in the middle. German soldiers and the Russian soldiers were fighting. The German tanks were behind our house and the Russian tanks were in front of our house. The Germans were in the forest behind the house when they discovered tanks in front of our house, and we were caught in the middle of the battle. We could hear all the explosions.

It went on for three to four hours before the Germans captured the tanks and Russian soldiers. We found it hard to breathe. I've never felt so helpless and frightened and didn't know if any of us were going to survive. When it was all over and everything was quiet again, we got out of our cramped little space and were able to look out and see that if we had been able to get out of our escape door to the shelter, we would have been killed. Our escape shelter and the schoolhouse were destroyed, and many soldiers were lying dead in the road.

It was so cold, and the bugs were so bad at night we could not sleep because of them biting us. We had to sleep with the lights on to keep the wildlife out. There we were with barely enough food to survive and unable to sleep. We had no idea of how or if we would be able to survive. Then the Germans who relocated us, realized that we were farmers, which meant we should be put on farms to work to provide food for the soldiers.

This is where I met my husband, Philipp Walter. We knew each other for a short time before he had to report for active duty in Denmark. Philipp's job was filling the refugee cans with soup. We were provided with more nourishing soup because Philipp had a ladle with a long handle that would reach the bottom of the pot and get us more of the cabbage and potatoes. Because of that additional nourishment, my family survived.

Bertha and Philipp Walter

We were at this camp for a while. One day a man came and knocked on our door and said there was a little girl that was run over by a German army truck and was lying in the street. He wanted to know if we knew who she belonged to and I immediately knew it was my seven-year old sister, Holdine.

I ran out and found her lying in the street. I picked her up even though the soldiers told me to leave her, and I took her home and laid her on my bed. I wasn't going to leave her lying in the street. I cannot remember if we had a funeral. I don't know if we were able to bury my sister or not. My mother refused to ever talk about it. We needed to pack up everything and prepare to leave because the Russians were invading.

They were so close that we heard their tanks as they moved towards the camp. It was frightening to hear those big tanks rolling towards our camp knowing that they were Russian soldiers that would show us no mercy. We were nothing to them and they didn't care if they ran over us. We had to leave, so we gathered everything we had remaining as quickly as possible. We were refugees again but this time I was married, and I had a baby.

Note: Outside of my mother's story, when it was discovered that my mother was pregnant, my grandfather contacted my father's commanding officer in Norway, and arranged a marriage by proxy. This was a wedding where one or both individuals are not physically present and are represented by someone else. The actual date of the marriage was something that we have always debated. We're guessing somewhere in the summer of 1943. The actual marriage certificate has mysteriously disappeared. Hmmmm…

It was September of 1944 and once again we had to load our wagon with whatever we had remaining and leave…I had to drive the horses. My father tied a rope around the wheels for traction so we wouldn't end up in the ditch. Wherever we went there were wagons laying in the ditches and people didn't know what to do. There were hundreds and hundreds of wagons and trucks on the roads. The Russians just didn't care. They drove down the roads and if they killed people that were in the way, it was not important to them. They treated us like it was a sport to see if they could run us over.

Along with my father and mother, Lydia and I went to find my mother's family. We had nothing to eat. I resorted to feeding my baby as a bird feeds her babies. It was a terrible way to survive but she was too young to eat on her own so I would put bread in my mouth and chew it until it was soft and pliable and then feed it to my baby. It was late 1944 and Lydia was nine months old. We had no milk. We had no water – just cold wet snow. We had to keep moving or someone would push us down from behind and we would never get back up on the road again. Everybody was desperate to get away from the invading Russian armies.

We finally came to the village where my uncle lived and were able to find a little house to move into. With the help of the Red Cross, it was there that my sister and her five children were able to find us. We hadn't known where she was or even if she was alive or not. We didn't know if my brother was alive either because we had not heard from him in two years. We all moved into that little house together – my sister didn't have anywhere else to go.

The buses were no longer running and the trains…if you ran hard you could hop on while the train slowly moved through each village and you could get a train ride. We didn't have anywhere else to go until my sister remembered an address she had been given and was able to locate a place where they sold tickets and showed them a piece of paper with the name of a city on it and asked the seller if he knew of a city in Germany with that name, and he said "Yes." She was unable to get us tickets because she was short of money. She had to turn away.

Here she came with her five children and moved in with us. Food was very scarce. At five in the morning, we would get up and stand in a line for a loaf of bread. My sister's two children – one was two years old and one was three, and they both died of hunger. One died in the evening and one died during the night within hours of each other. We had no way to bury them, but the Red Cross helped us out. We buried those children and I said, "Now, who's going to be next?" I thought for sure my own year-old baby was going to be next. This was January of 1945.

I didn't know where my husband was, and my brother was still missing. Next door was a farmer and my sister asked him if we helped him milk the cows would he give us a little milk – we did that and that is how our children had milk.

We survived and we worked hard. My father helped and we were able to get through it. One day when I was at the train station, I heard a man calling out my name. It was my brother, Wilhelm. A month later, we were all in the house when I saw a man coming up the path and when I opened the door, I saw it was my husband, Philipp. He stumbled and fell flat on his face landing on the floor unconscious. He was in and out of consciousness for a long, long time.

When he was well enough, he said, "I'd like to go to Hamburg and see my family and want you to come along." The only transportation we could find was an empty coal car on the train, so we got on it and went to see his stepmother.

My father was unable to find a job in the village, so he decided to go to Stuttgart, Germany and send for us after he found work. He went and in a couple of weeks he sent for us and we all went to Stuttgart where we found shelter in a military barracks. There was no place else to live and he had to pay extra to move into the military barracks.

My parents were able to buy a bombed-out house with rooms missing walls. With the help of my husband and my brother-in-law, Adam, they rebuilt that house. I told my sister that I was going to stay in the barracks a little longer and let my sister, who had more children, live in the house. My parents lived on the first floor and my sister lived on the second floor.

You can see the dents where the bombs hit.

When they bought the house, they were so busy working that they didn't check everything. We had neighbor children that played hide 'n seek and because our house came right up to the sidewalk, as most houses do in Europe, the local children went in to play and by jumping down into the basement they landed on the gas valve and turned it on. We found my mother dead hours later. She had been in her room sleeping and the door and windows had been closed.

It was the only time that I wanted to give up. I didn't want to live anymore. It was just too much. Losing my grandfather and then my mother was more than I was able to comprehend. It brought me to my knees, and I didn't want to continue with this wretched life. I wanted a home for my children. Everything was so dark, so gloomy, and so hopeless. People were living on the streets. I was living in an old military barracks.

There was one time when we didn't have any money at all. Overnight the money changed and became worthless, so we didn't have any money anymore. We had a neighbor who worked in the mill bring us a ten-pound bag of flour on her way home. Another neighbor told us we could have all the fallen apples from their orchards. A man put money in my husband's coat pocket and with it we were able to buy oil for cooking.

My husband and my sister wanted to leave Germany and decided that the four of us with our children were going to America. The only countries accepting refugees in 1951 were Argentina, Sweden, and America. We had applied for sponsored immigration and were accepted by both Argentina and America, however, Philipp decided that we should try for a new life in America and so it was. We immigrated to the United States in November of 1951 on the MS Samuel Taylor with our destination being through New Orleans and a train to Texas. We had a sponsor in Texas way out in the desert.

The trip took approximately three weeks and after arriving at the docks in New Orleans we continued our travel to San Antonio, Texas where our sponsors, Mr. and Mrs. Jordan picked us up to take us to our new home near

Mason, Texas. I spent most of the time on the train crying because this new country was so vastly different from Germany. We passed through small towns and farming country which seemed primitive and so very isolated. Nothing was green with flowers. There were no trees and nothing inviting. Just stupid cactus that grew everywhere.

I was terribly upset one time when I saw one woman in her home pull her window up as our train passed by. I could not understand that the windows didn't open outward on hinges as they did in Germany. I had never seen windows that slide up and down. I thought that all of America was going to look like this barren state of Texas.

Note: This is where she ended her story. And this is what we know:

1. When they came to Texas, Lydia was seven, Rosemarie was four and I was not quite one.

2. They stayed in Texas from 1951 to 1953, the sponsors required a two-year commitment to work off the travel cost.

3. Karl was born in Texas in 1953.

4. Our family along with other families that had been on the MS Samuel Taylor decided to go to Colorado. The story is that they were taking a detour to Oregon and then decided to stay.

5. Our youngest sister, Heidi was born in Oregon in 1959.

6. My parents made a good life for our family in Oregon where they remained.

Chapter Six
Georg Walter's Family

I tried to find information regarding my dad's (Philipp Walter) family but there isn't a lot of background or information on my grandfather, Georg Walter. From different writings and memories from family members, I was able to piece a bit of history on him.

My grandfather, Georg Walter, was born in Tarutino, Bessarabia in December 1896 and christened (Lutheran) fourteen days later. Shortly afterward his family relocated to Ruschkanofka, Bessarabia, and there they were able to remain until his death. Georg Walter died on August 24, 1943, at 6:00 P.M., as was written on a local certificate issued but not recognized by the German Government until it was documented on May 5, 1944. Because of WWII, many things took a considerable amount of time to become official and legal.

Georg Walter met Katherine Walter (her maiden name was also Walter), who was born in 1894 in Bessarabia. This is where Philipp Walter was born in 1923 into a family who farmed the land. On his birth certificate his father, Georg, and his father's sister, Marie Walter, were listed as unmarried witnesses to the birth. This is the only photo I was able to locate that had my dad's family in it. With the help of several family members, we were able to identify most of the people.

In the back row is dad's half-sister Lisabet (Lise); next to her is dad (Philipp Walter). Second row is dad's half-sisters Maria, Katherine, Philippina, Karoline, stepmother Regina Hess, Father Georg Walter, and half-brother, Robert.

Philipp Walter was raised on a farm and was the oldest living child of Georg and Katharine. The first of their children died of pneumonia when they were young. Philipp also had a severe case of pneumonia, but his father, Georg, insisted that the doctor do everything he could to save him regardless of the cost. Philipp was three years old when his mother, Katherine, died.

Dad's father was so totally distraught and devastated by the death of his young wife, that he removed everything and anything from the home that had any connection to her and refused to even mention her name or anything relating to her. Any mention of her was strictly "verboten" (forbidden).

Georg married Regina Hess shortly after his first wife's death, which was not unusual because Georg had a farm to maintain and a three-year old son that needed to be taken care of. Dad always felt that his stepmother favored her own children which haunted and affected him his entire life. He didn't return to Germany for thirty-five years and then only went at my mother's insistence.

My father never had any desire to see his family. He lost all contact with his family during the war, but my grandfather, Heinrich Zorn, managed to track them down in Hamburg. I believe Dad visited them one time when he and mom went to Germany. I know he spoke to his half-sister, Karoline, and half-brother, Robert, via telephone on birthdays and holidays. I spoke to Karoline several times myself when she would call to talk to Dad. It was rather exciting to me that I was able to converse with her in German.

Georg and Regina had four children together that are listed on an "Einburgerungsurkunde" (naturalization) Document. His half-siblings resented Dad because he was the "favorite" child. Dad was Georg's firstborn son and became responsible for the daily milking and caring for the livestock on the farm.

He would be sent out to take care of the livestock just before dinner time and his stepmother, Regina, would serve dinner as soon as he left. By the time he had finished his chores, dinner would be over, and everything was put away. His half-sister, Karoline, was kind and would put aside food for him so he would have something to eat when he was done with his chores. He always spoke of her with great affection. Karoline remained in contact with dad up until the time of his death.

It was not until Dad was ninety-four that I found a photo of his mother through a DNA source and was able to print a copy and take it to him. I asked him if he knew who this person was. He shook his head and said he didn't recognize her.

I said, "Dad, that's your mother." He was speechless and stared at the photo and then the tears came. He said that he had never seen a photo of her before and had always wondered what she looked like. He spent his whole life not knowing what his mother looked like and anything about her. Neighbors had told him that she was "quite the looker" and a very thoughtful and kind woman who had adored her son. He thanked me over, and over again for finding the photo of his mother.

Katherine Walter

Chapter Seven
Philipp Walter

WWII

Author's Notes: Dad's story was pieced together from conversations with him, documents, research into WWII and writings I had accumulated over the years that were about him.

Germans were required to always have their ID papers on them. Dad's ID was linen because paper wouldn't hold up with the constant folding and unfolding. During and right after the war, you were always asked "Ihre Papiere, Bitte" – meaning show the authorities your papers. Old WWII movies always make a reference to this.

In 1939 at the age of sixteen, Dad was drafted by the German army while he and his family were in a refugee camp in Poland. At that time, the draft was not for a specific period, but for the duration of the war, however long it would take.

Dad is on the left in the back row peeking between two soldiers – one in a dark uniform and the other a light uniform. Their commanding officer was straight on in the middle.

In April of 1940, Dad was sent to Denmark as part of Germany's preparing to move into Norway. Denmark felt it was necessary to set up radar systems to detect British bombers that were bound for Germany. Dad was stationed in Denmark for six months while preparing for the invasion into Norway. An interesting side note is that during this time, my older sister Lydia's future father-in-law was part of the Danish resistance underground movement.

It was during this time in Denmark that Hitler issued an order to confiscate all bicycles in Denmark knowing that bicycles were essential as a source of transportation for the Danish people. It was a huge blow for them.

Six months later, with Norway under German occupation and in an attempt to secure the harbors to control the North Atlantic, the army transferred Dad to Trondheim, Norway as an artillery gunner at the rank of Corporal (he had two V Stripes on his sleeve). As a soldier, Dad was proud to have earned this rank.

As an artillery gunner his job was to focus on any aircraft that was attempting to enter the harbor. He and his companions lived in trenches for four and a half years. These trenches were long, narrow ditches dug into the ground and were muddy, uncomfortable, and cold. They would flood in bad weather creating trench foot among the soldiers. Soldiers often lost fingers or toes to frostbite. Some soldiers died from exposure.

Even when they were not actively fighting, the soldiers were busy maintaining the trenches, moving supplies, cleaning their weapons, doing inspections and guard duty. Dad said he does not think that he ever hit anything because planes or ships never came close enough.

Dad is the fifth one over with his hand inside his shirt.

There was one time in late 1944 while in the trenches in Norway, Dad and his German comrades in arms, saw a German war ship being bombed by planes and they could hear the screams and see the hundreds of soldiers on board the sinking ship leaping into the ocean. He knew it must have been a German ship because otherwise it wouldn't have been attacked by the Allies. Dad said he and his fellow soldiers were helpless and could only watch and not be able to help because they wouldn't be able to save any of the doomed men and they also would have given away their position.

Dad recalled that it was horrible listening to the soldiers screaming and crying for help and unable to do anything to help them. They later learned it had been the Tirpitz being bombed by the British. The ship capsized and eventually sank, claiming the lives of more than 900 German soldiers.

He recalled another episode when he and a companion were being rowed back across the bay to their post in a small rowboat with two Norwegian fishermen. Halfway across Dad realized how easy it would be for the two fishermen to attack them and dump them overboard, seeing as how they were the enemy. He does not know why they didn't. Dad had a difficult time knowing that he was regarded as "the enemy" when he didn't want to be the enemy.

While in the trenches, the soldiers heard a lot about what was happening back in Germany, but they couldn't believe that the Motherland could possibly be capable of such atrocities. They thought it was just propaganda being broadcast by the Norwegians to dampen the morale of the German soldiers. They couldn't talk or discuss anything about the war or Germany amongst each other because they could not trust each other. If they did say anything and it was told to their commanding officer, they would immediately be shot by a firing squad. No questions asked.

It wasn't until a considerable time later that he learned the truth about what the German government had done to other people during the war. He didn't realize the magnitude and scope of what had happened.

During the last year of the war, Dad and his fellow soldiers were consistently told by the German authorities that Germany was winning the war. However, the soldiers were able to obtain a radio that they listened to undercover. The news they were hearing was from the European radio waves and the reports were of battles that were being won by the Allies. The soldiers knew that Germany was lying to them, but they would never speak of it to each other for fear that they would be "ratted" on by their fellow soldiers to the German authorities.

When they heard on the radio that the Americans had joined the war and were now landing in Europe, they all knew without any doubt that Germany was losing the war and it would finally be over. In April of 1945, Dad's regiment was cornered with Norwegian forces and Allied armies on one side and the mountains and the sea on the other.

Germans occupying Denmark surrendered on May 5, 1945 and effective at midnight on May 8, 1945 they surrendered in Norway. There were approximately 400,000 German soldiers in occupied Norway at the time of the surrender.

The night before their surrender their commanding officer gathered them together and told them they were going to be surrendering to the British first thing in the morning. Their officer advised the soldiers that were not from Germany itself but from German occupied territories (such as Bessarabia) to let their British captors know. Those soldiers, including Dad, were separated, and received better treatment as POWs than the men that were directly from Germany. Dad didn't mention where these interrogations and POW camps were, however, all documentation indicates they were in Western Europe. However, there were internment camps in Norway and many German POWs lost their lives to exploding bombs at the camps after being forced to criss-cross across mine fields. All these camps were cleared of POWs by September 1946.

Dad's regiment was turned over to the British and released to the Americans as POWs where they were divided into different groups for interrogation and release purposes. There were seven interviews each soldier had to go through before their release. These interviews were held in a large tent with seven tables staged with American officers at each table. The American assigned officers that were able to speak fluent German.

Each table had a different officer asking the same or similar questions in a different way that were asked by the previous interrogator. They were trying to confuse the prisoners into "confessing" at the number of casualties there were at the hands of the Germans. By the time they got to the last table for the last interview all the notes from the previous interviews were there waiting, which surprised Dad at how fast and organized they were.

After a few of the interviews, the prisoners knew what to expect. One of the questions Dad was constantly asked in different formats was how many deaths he was personally responsible for. His answer remained the same – that he didn't think there were any. He was never stationed at the front and never participated in an actual battle or any type of confrontation.

After the interrogations, Dad's group were given sleeping bags and were put into a tent community in Norway. They had to sleep on the ground which was frozen in the beginning but thawed as time went by, turning the ground into mud. As POWs, their American captors didn't treat them as well as the British did and didn't provide the POWs with enough food and many of them died from starvation and various illnesses.

Dad said that he only had a big piece of cardboard, as did many of the other POWs, to help insulate them from the frozen cold ground. If they left to go anywhere, they needed to find someone to guard their cardboard from being stolen by another POW.

After piecing together what information was available, it was determined that Dad was a POW from May 8, 1945 to sometime in September 1945. He was twenty-three years old.

THE WALTER FAMILY

1960

Chapter Eight
Eulogies from Philipp Walter's Funeral Service

February 2019

Eulogy Written by Lydia Walter Jensen
Read by Lydia's youngest son, Lars Jensen

I am so sorry that I am unable to attend our dad and grandfather's memorial today because I am overseas and can't get back to the States. I would like my youngest son, Lars, to share with you a few words from me.

Our dad had many challenges in life. Dad lived in four different countries during his lifetime. In Europe he traveled on horseback and carriage drawn by horses. In America he drove vans, cars and flew in airplanes. He spoke three or four languages. He saw Neil Armstrong land on the moon. He watched our first black-and-white television and listened to the radio. He stopped using money orders when our brother showed him how to write checks.

He worked hard all his life, primarily in the beginning to save money so we could live in our own house. A man who never backed away from a bit of extra work to help his children because he believed that we each had to own a house. He was quiet with a strong spirit and will. He observed life and people which often brought a chuckle and twinkle to his eye when he thought no one was watching. He was a loyal father who provided for his family.

I would like to share a couple of memories of our dad. After arriving in America, his first motor vehicle was a pickup. The first time I drove with my dad, he didn't quite manage the curve on the country road, so we ended up bouncing along in a cow pasture in Texas. Once he learned to round those curves, he decided it was time to get his license. I was eight years old at the time.

Off we went to the little town of Mason, Texas, where I presented my dad in my best third grade English and informed the sheriff that my dad had come for his "like-kan-see" test. Neither my dad nor I knew how to pronounce the word "license."

With a smile the sheriff took dad for his driver's test through the only main street in Mason, with me in the backseat translating – "turn right, turn left, park, shift into reverse, shift the car back into drive, now head back to the sheriff's office." We were both happy when we learned that dad had passed the driver's test. We lived in the wild west so there was no written test. I mean, if you could ride a horse, you could drive a car.

The town of Mason had hitching posts for the ranchers' horses, a feed and general store, and elevated wooden sidewalks with wooden steps leading up to them.

I am sure the driver's test was an unusual experience for all three of us – Dad, the sheriff and me. Dad and I laughed all the way home and congratulated each other – me for having managed the English and dad for passing the driving test.

I was so happy when my brother, Karl, landed in the Walter family. Finally, I could stop being the oldest "son" and let my brother take over for me. Unfortunately, he was still too young to help, so dad and I built the garage, and dug out the soil to extend the basement in the evenings after work. Dad taught me to use a hammer, a screwdriver, and a saw. I was relieved not to have to learn how to do electrical wiring, plumbing and carpentry. Those were my brother's challenges when he took over. Thank you, little brother and thank you, Dad.

When I turned fifteen, Dad decided it was time for me to learn to drive. He picked me up from work one Friday evening – I was working at the Fabric House in the Lloyd Center at the time – gave me the keys to the car and said, "You are driving home." Off we went and I drove thirty miles an hour on the freeway in the emergency lane. What can I say? Our dad was an optimist. He never gave up. He was humble, determined, and encouraged us to always try.

We learned to take responsibility and had chores which our mother set up and Dad enforced. I helped with the cooking and washing the dishes. Trudy learned to peel potatoes and cook pasta. If you wanted to eat meat, you also had to eat potatoes or pasta. Another sister swept the floor and dried the dishes after every meal. We had a clean house.

Our younger brother spent time in the basement making root beer which sometimes entertained us when the bottles exploded while we were having dinner. Dad liked the root beer and really supported that project. Our youngest sister came along later in life and was the child that was adored by Mom, Dad, and all the siblings.

When things were difficult in our home, Dad hunkered down and tried, to the best of his ability, to resolve matters. Times were tough sometimes. We certainly were not indulged or pampered. We ate what we were served, tried to do well in school and learned what good manners are. As I said, sometimes things were strained at home and Dad had to step in. Whether with a slap or words, he created order and brought the situation under control.

Thinking back on the challenges our parents had in their lives, I think our dad coped as well as he could. I think he cared for us but was not always able to express his feelings. His childhood was harsh, so his gentleness was not always evident.

I think we can all say, "Thank you, Dad, for all your patience and hard work in providing for us. Thank you for trying to understand and care for us." We will miss you, as you have taught us many lessons in life which we have gratefully incorporated into our own lives. Our parents left us with a heritage which we can pass on to our children and grandchildren. A heritage of which we can be proud and for which we can be thankful.

Trudy Walter Carlson

Eulogy Written by Heidi Walter Schweitzer

Dad filled many roles in his ninety-six years. He was a son, a brother, a husband, a father, a grandfather, and a great-grandfather. He was a farmer, a soldier, a POW, and a house painter. But if you ask anyone who knew him to describe him, they will say he was brave, hardworking, honest, a kind man, and indisputably, a man of faith. He bravely brought his wife, Bertha, and three little girls from his war-torn German homeland to the United States and the open spaces of Texas.

He worked for two years on a ranch, learning to communicate in an unfamiliar language so he could provide a better life for his family – a family that now included a son. After relocating his family to Oregon, apparently a slight detour since they were supposedly on their way to Colorado. Dad and his family connected with a church that helped his family get settled in their new community with housing, food, and a job as a house painter; a profession he continued for over thirty-five years. He was a hard worker, often working six days a week painting houses, and he was able to save and purchase a home for his family in NE Portland, a home that greatly benefited from Dad's ability to remodel.

This home bears the memories of the neighbor across the street and some dispute over the ownership of apples and whose side of the street they should fall on. The neighbor would stand in the middle of the street and throw the apples that had rolled onto her side. There was Mrs. Zicha giving Lydia, Rosemarie, and Trudy piano lessons in exchange for mom cleaning her house and memories of endless cabinets and shelves with her salt and pepper shaker collections that needed dusting. Then there was going next store to Mrs. Rulifson's house to watch Shirley Temple movies on Sunday night. Saturday morning it was off to another neighbor's house to watch cartoons.

While in this residence the family also grew one last time with the addition of our youngest sister (Heidi), the self-proclaimed favorite. In his last years, our youngest sister would visit her father and remind him she was his favorite. He would get an impish grin on his face and say to her "you're all my favorite," but we all knew he had to say that.

A few years later Dad sold that home and purchased a home in SE Portland where the remodeling restarted, piano lessons continued, and the kids snuck next door to watch *Dark Shadows* and *Batman*. Here they built new memories of holidays and celebrations, began traditions, and lived for over forty years.

Dad modeled honesty and integrity to his family. He taught all his children to work and how to save their pennies. Once a month on a Saturday the family would head to the big Goodwill in downtown Portland. He gave each child fifty cents to buy whatever they wanted. It was a rare treat to get money.

Not surprising, as she was and still is an avid reader, Trudy usually bought books. Dad would occasionally surprise his children on a hot summer evening by coming home with a jug of A&W root beer and a brick (yes, a brick; ice cream was in a square brick) of vanilla ice cream for floats. The family would line up on the porch to enjoy the treat in their Tupperware glasses and tall spoons.

The beach was one of Dad's favorite places. He never had paid vacations or holidays but during each summer, on a Saturday morning, Dad would load up the kids, all their paraphernalia, the cat and her kittens, and the Dachshund named Schatzie into the car and drove them to Seaside. It was exciting when he honked the horn when we drove through the tunnel which was halfway to the beach.

There Dad would spend the weekend painting and doing repairs on a family friend's beach house in exchange for rent. He would leave his family there on Sunday night then go back to Portland, work during the week and return the following weekend to bring his family back home. That was his vacation, and he never complained.

Dad loved his family and would do anything for them. Whenever any of them needed help he was right there with his overalls and his tool belt to give a hand. He worked alongside his son and sons-in-law, teaching them how to use a hammer, a saw, and, of course, a paintbrush. He hated to stop working until the job was done and often outworked those who were half his age. He wouldn't take the easy way. He wanted it done right.

He ate mountains of popcorn and consumed sunflower seeds until his tongue was numb. He loved chili with Fritos and vanilla ice cream. But his favorite treats were pumpkin pie and donuts. Our brother would often bring him pie, chocolate bars, and donuts in those last months. He usually said "no, thank you" (he was so polite), but if you placed a donut and a cup of coffee in front of him, he'd get a little grin on his face and they would be downed in record time.

He took great pleasure in the simple things and was always so thankful. Even in the last days when he needed help eating, and it was difficult to speak, he would say thank you for every mouthful.

If you visited him, he would always thank you for coming and wanted you to tell your family (he listed each one) hello for him. He was a strong man of faith. For a man who had lost so much at a young age, it was amazing he was never bitter. His belief in a Heavenly Father sustained him through many hardships as evidenced if you leaf through his Bible. He has many verses underlined and lots of papers with references that he had read. This verse was handwritten on a piece of paper and placed between the pages of his Bible.

Luke 10:27 "…Love the Lord your God with all your heart and with all your soul and with all your strength and with all your mind and love your neighbor as yourself." He modeled this every day of his life. If it was Sunday, we went to church. No discussion. If it was Wednesday, we were at Royal Rangers, Missionettes or Youth Group. He never said "no" if he could help. He gave whenever he could. Through his example his children were taught to be generous, kind, and forgiving.

Even though they often failed, there was never judgement. He corrected them, he disciplined them, but he always forgave them, and he loved them. Another scripture he had written out and placed in his Bible perfectly describes his character. Colossians 3:12-14: "So be gentle, kind, humble, meek and patient. Put up with each other, and forgive anyone who does you wrong, just as Christ has forgiven you. Love is more important than anything else." He loved his family. He loved spending time with them and enjoyed them.

He prayed for each of his children, grandchildren, and great grandchildren by name every day. He prayed for their salvation and their protection. He asked God to provide for them and bless them. And he expressed thankfulness that God had blessed him with each one of them. He often read and recited the 23rd Psalm in his daily devotion time. It was one of his favorite passages. It gave him great comfort and he often discussed how good God had been to him and how thankful he was. He didn't fear death because he knew where he was headed.

Chapter Nine
Lydia Walter Jensen

At the request of my sister, Trudy, I am going to write my biography to add to her ongoing project. I am the oldest of five siblings and, as of the date of this writing, January 2, 2008, sixty-three years old. I was born in Godendesfeldt, Westpreussern (Prussia). After me is a sister who was born in 1947 in Alten Ebsdorf, Germany.

My sister, Trudy, is next. She is six years younger than I am and was born in Stuttgart, Germany in 1951. My brother is nine years younger than I am and a true American. He was born in Kerrville, Texas in 1953. Heidi, the baby in our family was born in Portland, Oregon in 1959 and is fifteen years younger than I am. Like our brother, she is an American. We used to joke with my parents and tell them that it was a good thing they stopped moving and settled in Portland, Oregon or we might have had another addition to our family.

Family History

Little is known about my father's family. As I mentioned earlier, I think his family came from the Bukovina area. My father was the only surviving child of my grandfather's first wife who died in childbirth after having had twelve to thirteen still births. My grandfather remarried and my father had three step-siblings, Liese, Kalin, and Robert.

My Childhood in Germany

I remember nothing of this time, except a place in Ebsdorf, where we lived on a farm. The farming family there were very strange (according to my mother), and I was never to look into the eyes of their grandmother because she might put a hex on me. I remember the grandmother trying to talk to me, but I always ran away.

I also remember one day I was in the courtyard playing and when the rooster and the turkey attacked me, I screamed, and my mother came running and saved me. She told me later that she had seen the grandmother looking out of the window and that she put a hex on me and that was why the rooster and the turkey attacked me.

I didn't have a happy childhood, as my parents were strict, and my grandmother scared me. My grandfather Zorn was my salvation. He always protected me and looked after me. I was held responsible for my two younger sisters and whatever they did, it was my responsibility to look after them. We struggled to survive. My grandfather, Uncle Adam, Uncle Wilhelm (my mother's brother) and my father were always looking for bargains, extra work, and networking to find food, clothing, and housing. We had so little.

I remember one time they managed to buy a pig or two from a farmer. They brought these pigs home (or maybe the farmer delivered them) and they were slaughtered in the yard behind the apartment house. I will never forget how those pigs squealed and all the work that went into cutting up the meat, making sausages, etc. The lengthy discussions about dividing up the meat. It all went according to who had the largest family which, of course, was my Aunt Katherina.

During all this commotion I had to look after my younger sister. I was so intrigued with all the goings-on with the slaughtering of these pigs, I didn't see my sister trying to catch the cucumbers in this big tub. Suddenly she fell in and I could not pull her out, so I yelled for help. My mother came running and rescued my sister, but I got a terrible beating because my mother accused me of not looking after my sister properly. I remember sobbing and sobbing until I thought my heart would break.

My grandfather lectured my mother, took me by the hand and carried me down to the cellar where he had fruit stored. He told me I could pick out any fruit that I wanted. After my grandfather managed to console me and I stopped sobbing, I reached for the biggest pear – according to my grandfather. He laughed and hugged me and told me that he was sure I was feeling much better now. After that I always looked for my grandfather and spent as much time as possible with him.

Years later when I went back to Germany to visit my German family in that very apartment house. I spent most of the year in a small room in that apartment to be close to my grandfather. Again, he looked after me and I loved my grandfather for his kindness and his care. He was the only kind, caring person in my life as a child.

Both of my parents were extremely strict. When I look back, I do not think I ever really had a childhood. My young life, from the time my two sisters were born and then my brother, I had to work and take on a tremendous load of re-sponsibilities.

I remember Grade One in Stuttgart; it was in a suburb called Zuffen-hausen. We lived in a camp along with a lot of other Russian-Germans. We had a tiny apartment – two rooms. A bedroom which was always freezing cold, and I was never allowed to go in there unless my mother gave me special permission.

I have absolutely no recollection of where my sister and I slept – I think we all slept in the same double bed. We spent all our time in the one room which served as an "all room." There was a tiny kitchen and I do not remember any bathroom. I think we had to go outside. There were not bathing facilities, so my mother would heat up the water in a kettle and pots, pour it into a tub and we children took turns bathing. I do not know where or when my parents bathed.

Times were strange and very desperate, but we managed and, finally, with the help of our grandfather Zorn, found our way into Stuttgart. I have more memories from that time. Again, my grandfather made sure we all had a place to live. He bought an old, bombed out piece of land on which the ruins of a house formed a collection of bricks. Together with my father, my Uncle Adam, my oldest cousin Reinhart, and our grandfather, they built an apartment house with three small apartments.

My grandmother (Augusta) never recovered from all the terrors of war and became a very depressed, unhappy person. I was terrified of her. She looked haunted and I can remember her terrible temper outbursts, her yelling and wailing. Everyone in the family accepted her behavior and said it was the war. What could anyone do to help her. She lived with her demons.

The family joined a church and would sometimes have prayer meetings or church services in this "all room." My sister and I had to stay in a corner of the room and be quiet, or sometimes we had to go to bed early. My parents would often go out in the evening, either to my grandfather's place or my aunt's place. Sometimes they visited friends. My sister and I were often left alone then. We were terribly afraid.

Sometimes when we were all at home, my parents and their friends and family would recount the terrors of the journey (die Flucht) from Russia. There were many people in this camp and in the surrounding area who had terrible psychological damages because of the traumas of the war. People constantly related their stories about the terrors of the war. I learned to pray early in life as the only consolation and the only way of feeling safe was to pray to God to protect me from the evils of this war.

One night my parents were out again and left us at home. I think they took my sister with them because, like me, she was terrified at staying home. I remember sitting on the sofa for hours afraid to move because I thought something terrible might happen if I fell asleep. I think I sat like that until my parents and sister came home and then I was scolded for not being in bed!

The next morning my mother came in and announced that the neighbor man had hung himself outside our bedroom window. I think if I said that our parents were very insensitive to my needs and to my feelings of safety it would be an understatement.

I also remember long discussions my mother had with the mailman; whose father had committed suicide. The mailman said that his father came every night in his dreams and told him he missed him and was waiting for him. It was not long, and we had a new mailman because the previous one had gone to join his father. My mother told me this just as a matter of fact. Another death, another suicide – well that was life, wasn't it? She said that some people just could not cope after the war.

School was a nightmare as well. I had a Fraulein who always took great delight in either reprimanding or punishing me. Once for homework, she gave us each three or four sheets of colored paper from which we were to tear into bits and put on a tree trunk. It was fall and we were to create a colorful tree. I decided my tree should have large maple leaves, so I had large leaves.

When I proudly presented my picture which, of course, was quite different from all the others, I was severely scolded, had my picture thrown out, and had to stand in front of the class with my hands on my knees where I was bent over and received a good paddling with a paddleboard. I was humiliated, ashamed and hated that woman from then on.

When my mother took me to the school one morning to tell this Fraulein I wouldn't be coming to school anymore because we were immigrating to America, I didn't say a word to the teacher. She wished me well and my mother, as usual scolded me for not saying anything, but I didn't care that I got a beating. The only thing I could think of was that I would never have to see that darn woman again. I would have gone anywhere on earth to get away from that awful woman.

I had a hard time learning to read, so I memorized everything. I remember thinking that no matter what language I might have to learn in this America, at least I wouldn't have this Fraulein – and maybe, just maybe, I would learn to read.

Of course, there was a lot of drama when my parents told the rest of the family that we were moving to America. My grandfather begged my parents to reconsider, but my father had made up his mind and America it was to be. We sailed away on the MS Samuel Taylor.

I had a wonderful time on this ship. We met another German family who were also going to Texas. They had two sons who took me everywhere with them. Every day was an adventure with these two boys – who were around ten and twelve (I was only six). My parents were quite pleased that they looked after me as they had their hands full with my two younger sisters.

Lydia, Rosemarie, and Trudy

Somehow, I was never aware of either of my sisters being born. I was only three when the first sister came along so I was completely oblivious to her appearance until much later when she was around three and I was six. When Trudy appeared on the scene, I was again completely unaware of her. I remember my mother carrying and looking after a baby while on the ship and was not aware of Trudy until we reached the sponsor's ranch in Texas.

Chapter Ten
Trudy Walter Carlson

I am the third born child of Bertha and Philipp Walter. I was born in Stuttgart, Germany in January of 1951 and christened Waltraud.

My story begins when we moved to Oregon and the first home I can recall was on 56th and Everett in NE Portland. One of my earliest memories is of church members at Apostolic Faith Church on 52nd and Duke bringing us Christmas gifts. My dad was temporarily unemployed. My dad had a job with the railroad, and while at work was injured. He got a metal shaving in his eye, and years later it cost the loss of his eyesight in that eye.

I remember standing at the front door while church members arrived at Christmas with gifts and casseroles for our family. I was young enough to think that any time someone came to visit they would bring either Christmas presents or food. I hadn't started school yet and didn't speak English, but it was a wonderful memory; standing at the door alongside my two older sisters, welcoming people I didn't know who brought us treats.

Trudy Walter Carlson

I started kindergarten at the age of five at Mt Tabor Annex on 52nd and Stark. Mt Tabor Grade School where my two older sisters attended, was down the hill from the Annex. The grade school housed grades One through Eight. I walked by myself from 56th and Everett to Burnside Street and then Stark Street. Both Burnside and Stark are major busy streets with the school being a little over a mile from our house. At five years old it never occurred to me that this was unusual. It was what was expected of me and so I did it.

When I got to school no exceptions were made for my inability to speak or understand English. There was no translator, no special instructions or treatment. I had to figure it out on my own. My mother couldn't help any of us because her English was even more limited than ours. And since we only spoke German at home, other than church, she didn't have any exposure to English. It took me at least three years before I was fully able to communicate or understand what was being said.

I recall a time at Christmas when my kindergarten class was encouraged to bring one of their Christmas presents to class to trade with others. My present was a doll that belonged to my sister, Lydia, and I was so excited that it was passed down to me. I loved that doll. I took it to school with me the next day and nobody wanted to trade with me. It was a treasured gift and nobody wanted to trade their store bought brand new dolls with someone who had a used doll. I was devastated when I realized that they thought my beloved doll was a reject. The teacher was kind enough to make someone trade with me, however, the memory has stuck to me to this day. I was a child who didn't speak English and had a hand-me-down doll nobody else wanted.

I gradually realized that the culture in my home wasn't the same culture as the other families' homes in our neighborhood. One obvious difference was about the belief of Santa Claus. We did not believe in Santa Claus and had never even heard of him. We didn't celebrate on Christmas Day. Our Christmas observance began early morning of Christmas Eve day. We were impatiently waiting for Dad to get home from work while Mom was in the kitchen preparing the Christmas Eve dinner.

Once Dad got home, we were besides ourselves waiting for him to get changed into clean clothes and get ready for Christmas dinner. We dressed up for Christmas Eve and it was special. Christmas and Easter were the only times we got brand-new store-bought clothes. That was a real treat. Being the younger of three girls, I always got the hand-me-downs. First to Lydia, then to Rosemarie and finally to me.

Lydia, Rosemarie, Dad, me, Karl, and Mom

Our Christmas Eve started when we sat down and enjoyed a dinner consisting of hot German potato salad, homemade rolls, red cabbage, and baked ham. The only American concession to our dinner came years late was Jell-O with fruit cocktail. We gathered around the table and ate potato salad until we couldn't possibly have another bite. The potato salad was never put away, it stayed in the pot on top of the stove. We would go back to the pot for a spoonful of salad throughout the evening. Christmas Eve was the one time that there was always an abundance of food (at least it seemed that way to us).

For years we thought this was a German Christmas tradition, and it wasn't until a conversation I had with Mom more than fifty years later, that I mentioned this. She laughed and said "Oh no! It is a traditional Bessarabian wedding dinner!" We were all shocked. She had no idea that we thought it was a German tradition. I still maintain the tradition on Christmas Eve and on Easter and it has become a request at regular family get-togethers.

After dinner we all cleared the table and helped wash the dishes. Then we gathered in the front room to continue our Christmas Eve tradition which consisted of Dad reading the Christmas story out of his German Bible. It seemed to take forever to a kid waiting to open gifts. We then sang "Stille Nacht" and "O' Tannenbaum" in German ending with Dad giving a prayer for our family. (Again, the longest prayer ever to our impatient ears.) Finally, we got to open our presents.

We didn't believe in Santa Claus and we didn't know anything about Christmas stockings hung by the fire. Christmas was on Christmas Eve. Period. We never had Christmas stockings and had no concept of what or why they were necessary. Our presents would gradually appear under our tree as the days led up to Christmas. We always took turns opening our presents and admiring what each one of us received. Every Christmas we received a package from Germany from Grandfather Heinrich. It was always full of chocolates, German cookie, and an advent calendars with chocolate in the pockets. Nobody else in our neighborhood had an advent calendar or knew what it was.

On the coffee table there were always bowls of oranges, tangerines, candy, and cracked walnuts and we ate peanuts while we opened our presents. Afterwards, we left all our opened presents under the tree and went to bed and getting up early Christmas morning to play with our new toys and eat Christmas Eve's dinner leftovers. We didn't know or understand America's Christmas Day traditions and our neighbors certainly didn't understand our Christmas Eve celebration. It made us different.

There was one Christmas when my brother, Karl, was working at a print shop and we ended up with tons of Christmas wrap. Unfortunately, it was all the exact same pattern in four different colors. It was a snowflake pattern, and each sheet was printed in one of four colors. It was quite comical to see every single present under our tree with identical wrapping paper. It took us several years to go through our supply. Sadly, we didn't take a photo of it.

Over the years, the Walter Christmas tradition evolved with the addition of American spouses. I gave up my Christmas Eve to embrace Carlson traditions on Christmas Day, however, I still miss the traditional German Christmas Eve and it doesn't have the same feel on Christmas Day as when I was a child. I hang stockings now, but I still make the hot German potato salad dinner with accompanying red cabbage. It's now called "Christmas lunch" and served on Christmas Day. It's just not the same. I prefer the German version of Christmas Eve. My American tradition for Christmas Eve is now Chinese Food and a movie. I don't like the compromise.

That was the first of the many differences we had of celebrating holidays. Easter was another example. We had no idea of what or who the "Easter

Bunny" was or Easter baskets with colored eggs and chocolate bunnies. Easter was a time of celebration because of the death and resurrection of Christ and there was no exception whatsoever. My parents were appalled at the concept of reducing a sacred religious holiday to include an Easter rabbit. Eggs and candy were definitely not part of the package.

When I was young, I would hide in the bushes of a neighbor that always had an Easter Egg hunt for their children in their backyard. I was fascinated by the concept and didn't understand what was behind it. They knew I was there and were perplexed at my non-understanding of such an event but didn't chase me away. To me, Easter meant getting a special store-bought dress, white dress gloves, patent leather shoes, a corsage from my boyfriend to pin on my dress and attending a sunrise Easter service at Mt Tabor park. Bunnies and eggs were never part of the event.

Another note-worthy American tradition that was not part of our culture was the Tooth Fairy. Say what? She left money under our pillow? Why? That was something we did not know and certainly did not understand. With that realization I was even more aware that our family traditions and culture were not in line with what Americans were used to and accepted. The same could be said of St Patrick's Day, April Fools, May Day, etc. We didn't initially celebrate Thanksgiving either. If it wasn't German, it didn't happen in our household.

Our mother was the only one in our neighborhood who baked their bread. It was a weekly event, and we would fight over the coveted heel of the fresh loaves when they came out of the oven. We got good at cutting off one end of those warm loaves and turning the loaf around so mom couldn't see what we'd done. She was on to us though and we got caught every time!

Making homemade noodles was also a regular event. Mom covered our dining table with large thin dish towels or a bed sheet and laid out the dough that she had made that morning before cutting it into strips to dry. Pancakes in our house were the German version and were made of eggs, and shredded raw potatoes and fried. They were served with homemade applesauce. The first time I made them for my family, my son Jesse covered them with ketchup and I was appalled! Ketchup! NO! I still haven't forgiven him for that.

We never had store bought cookies but had fantastic homemade cakes and desserts. One of our favorites was mom's streusel cake with Italian prunes on top. Most of our desserts involved fruit. They were always dense without icing or cream filled. My mother would say that store bought cake and bread was poofy and full of "luft" (air).

We did a lot of canning and nobody else in our neighborhood did that. While other kids were out playing in sprinklers, riding bikes, or tossing balls, we were peeling tomatoes and pears, and snapping beans to be canned. We were up in trees picking cherries and apples. We had big crocks full of pickles or sauerkraut sitting on the kitchen floor. We didn't always wait for those pickles to age and would sneak one before they were ready. We made our own root beer which was always a disaster but the only soda we ever got for years. We would be having dinner upstairs in the kitchen listening to the bottles exploding. Mom made all our jams. We didn't know that any of this was unusual. This was our norm.

We never had a lot to eat and I had no idea how poor we were because we never went hungry. Mom grew up on a farm and had lost so much during WWII that she was able to make a meal out of anything. We thought everybody ate Zwieback toast with hot milk. Our favorite was bacon fat spread on a piece of bread with salt. Rice cooked in milk and sprinkled with cinnamon sugar was a treat.

We always had clean clothes and our home was always clean. Our clothes were rarely new and we thought going to Goodwill on a Saturday to pick out clothes and shoes was exciting. Dad gave us a nickel or a dime to spend on whatever we wanted. I always managed to find a used book to read.

We had our church clothes, school clothes and play clothes. We were never allowed to interchange any of them. We weren't allowed to wear pants until years later. It was against the church doctrine. We weren't allowed to wear pants to school either, but that was the dress code back then at the high schools. We weren't allowed to wear pants or shorts (it had to be "pedal-pushers" which today are called capris) in public including our own front yard.

Our bicycles originated from trips to the local dump that my dad, Karl, and I would take. We always came home with all kinds of treasures that were repurposed into useful toys and household items. I loved those trips. Farm living and WWII taught our parents that nothing should be wasted.

We were never allowed to enter our house through the front door and the living room was off limits. It was only for company. It was always immaculate and fortunately we were spared the plastic covers on the furniture. We did have plastic covers on the rugs in the hallways though. It was great for sliding on in our socks. We always came in through the back door and took our shoes off before entering the kitchen. We didn't have a television and went to a German family's home to watch the John F Kennedy funeral. Our church forbade us to have a television because it was a "box of the devil." When we finally did get one, it was hidden in the basement for us to watch in secret. Eventually it made it upstairs to be hidden in the front coat closet, but never to the living room. It made its appearance only after most of us had left home and my parents' downstairs bedroom became the "TV room". None of this seemed strange to us but it made us the source of ridicule.

We snuck to the neighbors' to watch forbidden shows like *Dark Shadows* and *Batman*. It was exciting when the neighbors got a color TV. When I was younger, I discovered my neighborhood friends watched cartoons on Saturday in the morning and I would always try to find a reason to go over to watch *Betty Boop*.

When I started going to Kindergarten at Mt Tabor Annex, someone told the school my American name was Violet. I was unable to speak or understand English when I started school and I didn't realize that she had done that. Mom didn't speak English either, so I have no idea where she came up with that name! I like my German name which is unable to translate into English unless you're good at spitting. It's Waltraud and the "W" sounds like a "V", you roll the "traud", so it sounds like you're clearing your throat, and pounce on the "D" sounding like a "T" (trout). That name didn't work out very well in Kindergarten and still is a challenge.

I changed my name when I was in the third grade because nobody could pronounce my German name, I didn't understand why I was called Waltraud (nickname was Traudel) at home, and among friends, and called something else by the teachers at school. Everybody else in my family had a German name that could be converted to English except for me. A few years later, when I was in the third grade, a young couple who lived around the corner from us had a baby and they named the baby "Trudy." I thought that was a wonderful name and decided it was going to be mine. It worked better and made more sense.

I went to school the next day and refused to answer to Violet or write that name on any of my class assignments. I was called to the front of the class and chastised by my teacher insisting that "Trudy" was not my name. She made me stand up there for what seemed like a long time and when I told her I had to go to the bathroom, she refused to let me go. I ended up wetting my pants in front of the class. I was mortified but continued to insist my name was "Trudy." How embarrassing – but I remained adamant.

I was sent to the Principal's office, who called my mother to make sure she would "straighten me out"; however, my mother didn't speak enough English, so that didn't work. Eventually I became Trudy. I love my German name, but I prefer to have it pronounced properly. This experience quickly taught me that I could get away with a lot because of my mother not speaking English. Eventually the school staff discovered I had two older sisters in the same school and one of them, Rosemarie was only too happy to tell on me every chance she got. She was – and still is – such a goody-two-shoes.

Both of my parents always worked hard, long hours and taught us to do likewise. Chores were expected as part of our structured lives. Every Saturday early in the morning my mother would have opened all the windows saying we needed "frische luft" (fresh air). We would wake up to having our blankets yanked to the ends of our beds and her shouting "Aufstehen! Aufstehen! Aufstehen" (translation get up!) This would be accompanied by the radio being on full blast to her favorite Christian music channel while she was singing along. It was so annoying. Saturday mornings in our household did not include bowls of cereal while we watched cartoons. We were expected to do chores and playtime was later in the afternoon.

At the end of the day we took our weekly bath with Ivory soap. To this day I refuse to have Ivory soap in my house. Heidi still hates the smell of Ivory soap. Lydia, being the oldest, always had the first bath, followed by Rosemarie and then me. We didn't have the luxury of a fresh bath, and we could add a few inches of hot water only if necessary.

Our mother was strict and quick to discipline. From what I understand of her own childhood this was the German way of child rearing and she continued this with her children. There was a definite lack of physical or verbal affection in our home which was also a typical German trait. We didn't observe any affection in other German families' homes either. My observation has been that as adults, my siblings and I have made the conscious choice to show our children lots of love and affection.

My parents, embracing a typical German trait, were always punctual and taught us to be the same. We were always at least five minutes early for any appointments and it would be considered offensive to have arrived late. We quickly learned that we were expected to strive for perfection and precision in our lives. Anything less was unacceptable.

Having been raised as part of a large German community, we found that our parents were not all that unusual as most Germans rarely admit having any faults, even jokingly, and even more rare that they handed out compliments. For us it was a way of life and we didn't understand why others found our attitudes to be unfriendly and unemotional. As an adult, a simple thank you was completely adequate and acceptable and, as a result, I have often been criticized for not being overly effusive in my thanks or compliments. It is difficult to acknowledge my children's accomplishments.

I started piano lessons when I was in the first grade and for the next twelve years, I had to practice for an hour every single day. I could hear the neighborhood kids having a great time outside while I was pounding away on the piano keys. I hated it. After I was done practicing it was time to help set the table and get ready for dinner. Dishes and then homework. Boring. However, I continued piano lessons until my thirties and studied music at Portland State University. I still enjoy playing the piano to this day unless somebody thinks they need to talk to me while I'm playing.

I credit those years with teaching me the discipline of finishing a task. I would start out with a new piece of music playing one measure at a time with the right-hand. Then when that was perfected, I would play the left-hand part of the same measure and continue until I had it perfect before combining the two and moving on to the next measure. I never looked at the entire sheet of music but worked on one measure at a time until the entire score was completed.

I have continued that practice throughout tasks and challenges I've had in my formative years. I view a problem that seems daunting and try to imagine the absolute worst thing that could happen. Once I figured out what the worst thing would be, then it doesn't seem so daunting anymore and instead becomes a challenge. I would break it down and tackle one thing at a time and I always had a Plan B.

We weren't accepted or made to feel welcome in America even after becoming citizens. It was quite the opposite. We certainly didn't feel entitled to anything. We worked hard and earned everything we had. My dad brought us to America for freedom and opportunity. Dad was so disgusted about what had happened to his homeland and was motivated to bring his family to America. We learned to never take anything for granted. He worked hard to achieve goals he would never have been able to achieve in Germany. He viewed his responsibility to vote as a privilege and always cast his ballot. In fact, how he voted was the one thing he refused to share with anyone, especially my mother. Made her crazy.

In our younger years, Sundays were set aside for church. Our routine was to go to church every Sunday morning, spend the afternoon visiting German families, being served coffee and cake with the family using coffee sets that were brought from Germany. Mom's set was one of her most prized possessions and was given to her by her father in Germany. It was brought out only on Sundays when company arrived. We were never allowed to touch the china which excused us from having to wash them.

Every week without fail, we went to church on Sunday morning. We went back to church on Sunday evenings, and we went to the Apostolic Faith location in downtown Portland on Tuesday and Friday evenings. For years there was an enormous rotating sign around the building that said "Jesus is the Light of the World." Even when the downtown location was closed, the sign remained along with a three-story lit white stag advertisement. On Friday nights during Rose Festival season, church leaders would go down to the harbor and bring back a dozen or more sailors from ships that were at the dock. They were all seated at tables in the church basement and served cake and coffee. As a teenager, I always managed to find a way to check out those sailors before being caught and sent back upstairs.

On Sundays we attended the Apostolic Faith Church location in southeast Portland, and I loved going and being in the huge tabernacle with the big dome ceiling and pipe organ. I loved the sound of the pipe organ coming from above high in the rafters. At Christmas time when the congregation sang "Angels We Have Heard on High," the church choir would be up in the rafters and to my mind it was angels really singing. It was glorious.

As young children we would dress in white robes, have wings made from gold tinsels and carry a flashlight with a red crepe cover to look like candles.

We'd line up on both long aisles and walk down to the front singing. It was magical and something I looked forward to. During the Christmas holiday, we were loaded into church buses and went to nursing homes to go caroling. It was fun when I was young but not so much as an adult. We gathered back at the church for hot chocolate and a brief service while our parents came to pick us up.

During all services, families sat together with smaller children. Teenagers sat with their friends and the boys sat on one side of the huge tabernacle and girls on the other. We were scrutinized and called out if caught even looking at the boys. I had a big flat corduroy purse that was the perfect size for a *Nancy Drew* or *Hardy Boys* book. I could sit behind a pillar in the back of the church and put my book inside the hymnal. My mother would glance back to check on me but I was always sitting very still and behaving. If the service was lengthy I was able to finish an entire book. She was probably so relieved that I wasn't causing trouble that she didn't pay attention to what I was doing back there.

During three weeks in July, we went to Revival meetings at the tabernacle three times on Sunday and then every evening for those three weeks. I loved those revival hell fire and brimstone revival meetings and have nothing but good memories of that church and those revival meetings every summer. The wooden sides of the tabernacle would be raised up with ropes to let in the cool air which I thought was wonderful. It was almost like being outdoors. The afternoon and evening services were my favorites. Instead of the typical Sunday morning service of a long sermon with lots of pounding on the pulpit, members of the congregation would stand and give their testimony.

While they were testifying, the chorister would put the number of the next hymn on a big board and in between testimonies the congregation would break into a song. I loved those meetings on a hot summer night with the sides of the tabernacle opened and locked into place letting in a warm breeze.

Dad, Mom, Heidi, and their friends at the campgrounds.

During camp meeting it was also an opportunity for my mother to take a strong hold on my skinny little arm and march me up to the platform where at least twenty different ministers (I'm sure that's an exaggeration but it seemed like there were that many) were seated and waiting.

These ministers would then form a circle around me and, while laying their hands on my head, demand that the Devil take the wickedness and rebellious nature from me. This happened at least once, sometimes twice, during every three-week revival camp meeting. I was ten years old. This was not one of my fonder memories.

An Official Teenager

When I was fifteen, I was able to get a work permit and went to work for a famous German restaurant in NE Portland called the Rheinlander. I was hired because I spoke German and the owner wanted someone to be authentic and could talk to patrons. That worked until I apparently talked to the patrons too often and I ended up getting fired.

He also didn't like knowing that I understood everything he said. He had enjoyed the anonymity of speaking in German to his buddies knowing that his employees didn't understand what he was saying. He decided he didn't want any Germans working for him anymore.

Years later I had another job working as a receptionist at a huge outdoor furniture store located at the end of the Burnside Bridge in Portland, Oregon. I was there for almost two weeks when I noticed the owner was being peculiar whenever he looked at me. A few days later, the owner called me into his office and was visibly shaken when he said that when he hired me, he knew I was from Europe, but he thought I was Danish. I had blue eyes, blonde hair and was fair skinned so he had assumed that I must be Scandinavian. He started asking questions and soon discovered that I was German and that my father had been a German soldier in WWII. He accused me of lying to him and I was shocked and protested. I never would say I was Danish! I never hesitated to say I was German.

My boss could not handle my presence and became very agitated and distraught and terminated my employment. He was so upset and apologized repeatedly, saying that he was unable to "function" knowing he was paying me a salary when I was German and his family, being Jewish, had been persecuted and murdered by the Nazis.

My response was that I didn't understand because I didn't have anything to do with what had happened to his family in Germany. I was incredulous that this grown man would be so upset at the sight of me. He said he knew that I could sue him for discrimination, and he wouldn't blame me if I did. I told him that I would manage and get another job and I felt extremely sorry for him that he saw me as part of the enemy. He was about to burst into tears, so I quickly left his office and went home. I sat in the back of the bus and cried. I was eighteen.

During my freshman year at Franklin High School my parents started attending First Assembly of God Church on 20th and Hawthorne in SE Portland. Once again, I enjoyed the structure and fellowship of belonging. This denomination had less fire and brimstone but included a lot of loud praying and speaking in tongues. I was part of a group of approximately fifteen other teenagers from different high schools and we all attended First Assembly of God.

It was a very tight social group and was an integral and vital part of my teenage years. On Sundays we would gather in a large house that was called "The Tucker" house and have Sunday school in the living room of the house. Afterwards we would walk over to the church for the Sunday church service.

Every Wednesday was youth day and we'd come from different high schools all over Portland and gather at the Tucker House to do homework together or, if the weather was nice, we'd go to a park a block away and hang out. At 5 P.M. we'd go to the church basement where we'd gather for dinner and for a youth group service while our parents would attend a service in the main sanctuary. It was a wonderful time and we had banquets where we'd be escorted by our "date" and wear prom dresses and corsages. It was magical and I didn't want it to ever end.

Every summer we would get bused as a group to a youth camp where we stayed for a week. At camp during our evening services, my friends would always speak in "tongues", but I was not able to do so and just recited poems and prayers I knew in German. I am not sure I fooled anybody because it was structured and unemotional and everybody else's was overly dramatic and emotional. I couldn't fake that!

It was a happy time for me and included my first serious boyfriend, Jack Dickinson, whose parents didn't approve of me because my family were immigrants who spoke German and weren't in the same social class as they were. I didn't care because this was my first boyfriend that was not German. My mother constantly told me it wouldn't last because I was not good enough for him.

I believed her because some of the adults at this church would refer to me "as one of *those* (emphasis on those) German immigrants" and was occasionally referred to as a "dirty little German." Some of my "friends' parents would say that I would never amount to anything and I was nothing but trouble.

They would often say these things in my presence which was strange because it was as if they thought that because I spoke German and was an immigrant, I didn't understand English or couldn't hear them. It was unbelievably hurtful and degrading and the die was cast. I was sixteen.

I also had my first real "best friend" at that church. Her name was Eileen Sanders, and she went to Grant High School while I attended Franklin High School clear across town. For the first time in my life I felt like I belonged to something special. Of course, mom didn't like Eileen at all. However, Eileen ignored her and stayed my friend. She was the first and only friend I had that was not intimidated by my mother. My mom would drive away any friends I might have had.

When we were in grade school, we never went to or had "slumber parties". It was unheard of and not permitted or even considered. There was one time that Rosemarie could go to a neighbor's house but that didn't end well. At 2:00 A.M. she was brought back home hysterical. That ended any future possibility for the rest of us.

Eileen was the only friend I had that could spend the night and that was only during the summer. Eileen would come over and spend the night and early the next morning we would walk down to the corner and get on the "berry bus" to go out to the fields to pick strawberries. It was usually cold and foggy and there were lots of slugs in the berry plants. Eileen always earned more money than I did probably because I ate more strawberries than I picked.

Eileen was also the only one brave enough to defy my mom. School friends were not allowed in our home unless they were German or because they weren't from our specific church. Eileen was the only one that my mother couldn't bully. I still stay in touch with her but not near often enough. Eileen was fourteen and I was fifteen.

A year or so later, when Jack broke up with me, my idyllic life came to a screeching halt. He dropped me off at home after our breakup. I was heartbroken because I was sixteen and it was my first serious relationship. Since he and his new girlfriend were part of the same social group at church that I belonged to, I was distanced from my friends. I was no longer included in the group gatherings because it was awkward for everybody – except Jack, of course. It was as if I no longer existed. I quit going to church which further validated their opinion of me. I no longer had a place there and no friends. I was always labeled as being a strange child, which I probably was due to my home environment and trying to find my footing in what was to be my life. I was extremely uncomfortable around any adults.

I didn't know that as you grow and progress in life, people come and go as circumstances change. I didn't know that this was a natural process and thought it was because there was something innately wrong with me.

My mother was very isolated at home with five children and it took her a long time to learn to speak English. I am sure she felt like she was no longer in control of anything – especially her teenage daughters – and didn't hesitate to exercise her anger and frustration on her children. She had no control over circumstances in her life and desperately wanted to maintain control and discipline over her children.

Since I refused to go to church anymore and seldom went to school, I no longer fit in anywhere. I left home at eighteen during my senior year of high school and lived a very nomadic and insecure life. I was a sheltered and extremely naïve young lady and started hanging out with a few neighborhood girls. I started going to parties even though I didn't drink alcohol and I wouldn't have recognized drugs if they were right in front of me. I was totally oblivious to the environment.

However, being in the "wrong crowd" I ended up pregnant as my mother had predicted I would. My bedroom was down in the basement and I tried to hide the pregnancy for months by staying down in the basement and getting up early with morning sickness hoping nobody would hear me. I would throw up in the washing basin and then rinse it so nobody would notice.

It didn't work out that way at all. My mom recognized the symptoms, and her reaction was to go to bed with a blanket over her head and lament loudly because I brought such shame on our family. She wanted to go back to Germany and leave this horrible desolate country. She was angry with me for bringing disgrace to her home and told me I had to find someplace else to live.

I moved in with a friend, Karen, who was a former neighbor, and school mate. Karen was at work all day and spent every evening with her boyfriend who clearly didn't want me there. I had to stay in the attic area where I slept on a cot and remained out of sight.

Early one morning in July, while Karen was getting ready to go to work, I went into labor. I didn't have a plan worked out about how I was to get to the hospital that was miles away. Karen said she could drop me off on her way to work if we hurried; otherwise, she would be late. She dropped me off at the entrance of the hospital and promised she would come back during her lunch hour to check on me.

I walked in and asked the lady at the information counter where the maternity ward was and then took the elevator up to the delivery floor where I informed the nurse at the station that I was there to have a baby. The nurses were stunned that here I was, a teenager, showing up unannounced and totally unprepared, all alone to have a baby.

I knew I was going to give the baby up for adoption but wouldn't sign the papers for the three days I was hospitalized because I didn't want to look back years later and wonder if I had been rushed into making such a monumental emotional decision. I recall somebody, probably the lawyer, came to my room within an hour after birth and handed me a pen and some papers to sign.

I wouldn't sign the papers. It was too soon. The next day my doctor came in because he thought everything was prearranged and was concerned about my not signing the adoption papers. He said that the adoptive parents had been notified and arrived that morning and were devastated that they had to go back home empty handed. I told him that there was never any doubt that I was going to sign but I just didn't want it to happen within an hour after giving birth. I needed more time.

I asked one of the nurses to take me down the hall where I could see the baby through the window. She asked me if I wanted to hold him and I said "no." I was unable to because I knew if I did, I wouldn't be able to give him up; it would be too heartbreaking. I had to give him up because I had nowhere to go and no one to help me.

Fast Forward Few Years

I ended up marrying Loren Sehorn, who was part of the "wrong crowd." He was everything I had been taught was wrong. He had long hair, rode a motorcycle, and smoked pot. I knew I was making the worst mistake of my life but wasn't about to back down. My mother had told me to choose between her and Loren. Duh.

When I started spending time with Loren, I met Nels Rurey because he was Loren's roommate. Years later I also met his girlfriend, Cindi but I didn't like either one of them. Cindi had me in her phonebook under the letter "B" for Bitch. Ironically enough and, despite our mutual dislike, Cindi and I became remarkably close friends.

Seven years later, she and Nels stood by me when I divorced Loren. My mom hated Cindi and called her a "snake in the grass" because she was my friend and mostly because she was not German. Why she thought my having a German friend would be different, I had no idea. I no longer knew any German girls.

Cindi and Nels Rurey were my steadfast supporters. Cindi was my Lamaze partner and was with me when my son, Philipp David, was born. I wanted a

"David" and wanted to honor my dad. David Philipp didn't have the right sound, so his name ended up being Philipp David and we called him David. Cindi and I are like sisters and bickered and loved each other like sisters. Fifty years later we are still exceptionally good friends, and she and Nels are still part of my family.

I took my maternity leave and decided I was not going to go back to work. It was unacceptable for me to leave my infant with a babysitter. I was collecting disability for a work injury and the insurance adjuster was a young man that wanted to help. He and his wife had just had their first child and his wife didn't want to stay home which upset him.

He was impressed that as a single mother, I didn't want to have someone else raise my baby. He was supportive and extended my disability pay for a few more months which gave me the time I needed to start a secretarial service to support myself and baby Philipp David. It became a good source of income for me and I was able to provide for and take care of Philipp David.

I started attending Sunday church services at a neighborhood Baptist church. Every Sunday after church, I did my grocery shopping at a local grocery store and during the week I would put Philipp David in his stroller and the two of us, with my dog, Ben, in tow, would go for long walks to get some fresh air. There's the "frische luft" business again. One of our destinations was a variety/grocery store a mile from my house. It was there that I met my future husband, Ernie. The first time he asked me out was for lunch; he was so nervous asking that I ended up finishing the sentence for him. I was impressed with him because he was nervous when other guys would have gone into their macho act.

Ernie was a real person and quite nervous around me. The more I got to know him the more I appreciated what a good man he was. He was a person who didn't talk up his religion but lived his religion. We dated for about six months before we decided to get married. I wasn't excited about the idea because I really didn't want to get married again or even be in a relationship, but I knew that it would be something I would regret if I didn't. I was quite content with being single and was annoyed when I discovered that I really loved this man.

I knew it would cause problems with my mom which was expected. I grew up without any relatives such as grandparents, uncles, aunts, or cousins and had managed so I knew could do it again but this time I would have a beloved partner at my side.

Ernie and I were married on the Sternwheeler on the Willamette River during the Portland Rose Festival in June 1989. We chose that because it was a neutral territory so as not to offend anybody by choosing a specific church.

My son, Philipp David, was four when we got married and Ernie had custody of his nine-year-old son, Jesse.

I was thirty-five when Philipp David was born, thirty-eight when Ernie and I got married. A year and a half later our son, Josef, was born and our family was complete. Being a stepmother to Jesse was complicated and challenging. I had absolutely no idea on how to cope.

I was now a parent to a four-year-old who had no respect for my opinions, a newborn, and stepmother to a nine-year-old. I had been single for a long time and a single parent for four years, and my life had been predictable and peaceful. I had no idea how difficult it was going to be to take on the responsibility of being the step-mother to a nine-year-old boy.

Those first few years of marriage were unbelievably stressful and tense. I had no idea of what unconditional love was until I had Philipp David and was coming to grips with what that entailed, and now I had a nine-year-old to raise and the only reference I had of being a parent was my mother. I was tossed into the deep end of child rearing without knowing how to swim. My German upbringing didn't permit me the luxury of being anything less than perfect.

In hindsight, I realize my "friends" and acquaintances did not, and still do not, understand that I was raised in a German culture and how it shaped me. It is part of who my parents were and is engrained in my DNA. It is who and what I am. I am aware that as a parent, I made a lot of mistakes. Some of which were cultural, some was DNA, and some plain trial and error.

As for me…I am married to my best friend and to a man who is honorable and steadfast. I have made a lot of errors in judgment and have tried, not always successfully, to move forward in how I treat my friends and raise my children.

Chapter Eleven
A Good Ending

In September of 2019, after forty-nine years of wondering and hoping, I decided that I was going to find the son I gave up. I put a lengthy post on my Facebook page telling the story of the adoption, who the father was, etc. and asked that it get reposted. I was amazed at how many times it was reposted and was encouraged at the numerous suggestions and offers of help that post generated. There were quite a few serious adoption organizations that offered their assistance to help find him but at the last minute I changed my mind.

It didn't feel right for me to pursue the search because I had no idea what his life was like and was reluctant to intrude with a "surprise, I'm here" scenario. Instead, I opted for taking five different DNA tests and if he were interested, he could find me. He did.

I received an email from him on December 26th regarding a DNA test saying that we were related. He was nervous and hesitant not knowing what kind of reception he would get. He didn't want to get his hopes up either. We were on vacation with my sister, Heidi, with unreliable internet. Since I had been doing a lot of genealogy and family history on-line, I assumed the notification was another distant fifth cousin – eighth removed! Especially because the notice from Ancestry.com said that for $19.95, they would tell me who was related to me. Heidi agreed with me. It was not until almost a week later that I remembered the email from Ancestry.com and read it. Then I looked at the DNA result and it said we shared DNA and were possibly related.

It took some emails going back and forth with me asking questions and him answering; questions with answers that nobody else could know – such as who handled the adoption and were his adoptive parents able to take him home right after the birth. By this time, the DNA results changed from "being related" to "being my son" and his name was David Scott. I was speechless and started crying so hard I could not breathe. I had gotten my David after all! I also discovered I had two grandsons.

The rest of the week was a blur of emotions. On Thursday, February 14, my youngest sister, Heidi, my brother, Karl, and I spent the entire day with my dad knowing it would most likely be his last day. He died on Friday morning and on Saturday we made the funeral arrangements. On Sunday I met my grown son for the first time. Wednesday was my dad's funeral. There were so many emotions involved that I could not process any of it. I was devasted at losing my dad and elated at finding not only my son, but a daughter-in-law and two grandsons.

The day of reunion was scary; my granddaughter informed me that a car was slowly going around the block and was now parked in front of our house. I was not sure what to do. My son, Dave, walked in the front door with a bouquet of flowers and it was as if we had never been apart. My youngest son, Josef, was here and seeing the two of them in the same room, there was absolutely no doubt that he and Dave were brothers. They are identical.

In June, Dave and his wife met two of my siblings and their families (a total of twenty-five people) and were totally overwhelmed. My older sister and her husband were visiting from Denmark and my youngest sister and her family came. I assured him that he was fortunate that it was only two of my siblings and not all four! I reminded him that I had forewarned him that he was related to a whole bunch of crazy Germans!

It has been a few years now since we reunited, and I could not ask for anything better. Dave is a wonderful man with a devoted wife and two sons. We have enjoyed a relaxing and comfortable reunion and have spent time with his family and look forward to continuing to do so.

Epilogue

I have made my peace with my mother and with the past and do not harbor her any ill feelings. When I was thirty, and newly divorced from Loren, I decided to accept the responsibility for my own life and actions. Blaming and resenting my mother for everything that had gone wrong was pointless.

Forgiving her does not mean that I will ever accept her actions nor does it mean that when you forgive someone your brain is wiped clean of the memories. For me, it only means I can remember the past without the pain and draining emotions. I can learn to make sure that I can be a better person and love my husband and my children.

I have also faced criticism for being straight forward and for saying "please" and "thank you" without a lot of emotion and fanfare and fuss. It is not part of my DNA, and flowery and gushing reactions are totally foreign to me. It is an emotion that I cannot relate to nor trust and makes me extremely uncomfortable to be around.

My four siblings have also had difficulties and issues having been raised in a strict German household but because of that, or despite it, we have succeeded in our personal lives and career choices. We all have a strong survival instinct, and it is what got us through those early years. We all have strong and loving relationships with our spouses and, with my being the exception, are still married to our original mates.

I never will hesitate to credit both of my parents for raising me with morals, integrity, and a strong knowledge of what is right and what is wrong. I recognize and am proud that a lot of my "traits" come from being of strong German descent. I have been unfairly criticized for looking angry. I am not angry – **this is my German face!**

Am Ende wird alles gut sein. Und wenn es nicht gut ist, ist es nicht das Ende.

Translation: Everything will be okay in the end. If it's not okay, then it's not the end.